COMPETING
IN THE AGE OF AI
AI LANDSCAPE
GOVERNANCE & SECURITY
GOVERNANCE & SECURITY
DATA READINESS
PILOT TO SCALE
UPSKILLING
TRADITIONAL METHODS
ADAPTABILITY
DATA INITIATIVES
RESKILLING
STRATEGY PATH
INNOVATION ROADMAP
INNOVATION ROADMAP
BUILD-VS-BUY
BUILD-VS-BUY

Competing in The Age of AI

The Hidden Truth About AI
&
The Fear of AI Taking Our Jobs

by

Sara Giovani

"When a business is driven by AI, software instructions and algorithms make up the critical path in the way the firm delivers value."

"Imperfect, weak AI is already enough to transform the nature of firms and how they operate."

"The fundamental idea behind the AI factory is to industrialize the company's approach to data, analytics, and artificial intelligence."

Preface

The fear of artificial intelligence displacing the human workforce is a central theme in the modern "Workforce Transformation." Current research indicates that while 69% of workers believe AI will lead to layoffs at their company, and 49% personally fear losing their jobs, the reality is shifting toward a model of job reshaping rather than simple replacement.

Based on the provided data and the architectural framework for competing in the age of AI, here is an analysis of how this fear compares to the emerging organizational reality:

1. The Job Reshaping Framework

The provided mind map identifies that most work will not disappear but will be categorized into three "Reshaped" roles:

- **Amplified Roles:** AI handles routine, data-heavy tasks, allowing the human worker to focus on high-value creative synthesis.
- **Rebalanced Roles:** The skill set shifts away from technical calculation toward "human-centric" skills like empathy, social reasoning, and ethical judgment.
- **Enabled Roles:** Entirely new categories of work are created to manage, train, and audit AI systems, such as AI Bias Auditors or Workflow Engineers.

Research suggests that over the next few years, approximately 50% to 55% of jobs in the US will be reshaped in this manner, while only 10% to 15% are projected for full elimination.

2. Identifying Vulnerable Categories

The fear of displacement is most acute—and most grounded—in "Vulnerable Categories." These typically involve standardized, measurable tasks that do not require a physical presence or complex interpersonal judgment.

- **Routine Knowledge Work:** Professional services and tech-adjacent roles (like basic legal drafting or entry-level coding) are seeing immediate impacts.
- **Standardized Manufacturing:** Roles that combine robotics with predictive AI systems are at higher risk of full automation.
- **Management Pressure:** Interestingly, 74% of senior managers expect AI-driven layoffs, as 80% report that AI has significantly increased expectations for their own output.

3. The Shift from "Replacement" to "Augmentation"

A critical component of the "Leadership Mandate" is moving the organization toward a "Human-In-The-Loop" model. This approach emphasizes that the most successful firms will not be those that replace humans with machines, but those that achieve "Hybrid Intelligence"—a partnership where AI handles "reckoning" (calculation and prediction) while humans provide "judgment" (ethics and context).

One surprising finding is that frontline employees who actually use AI in their roles report lower levels of burnout (41%) compared to those who do not (54%), suggesting that active collaboration with the technology can alleviate some of the stress associated with the fear of being replaced.

4. Competitive Insecurity: "The Person Who Knows AI"

The research highlights a new dimension of fear: 65% of frontline workers worry that they will be replaced not by a machine, but by a person who knows how to use AI better than they do. This has led to "Strategic Upskilling" becoming a primary defense. Future-built companies are now planning to upskill more than 50% of their employees to address this gap, compared to only 20% at organizations lagging behind.

Ultimately, while the World Economic Forum predicts a net increase of 78 million jobs by 2030, the transition remains a significant psychological challenge. Success depends on leaders who can move beyond "tool rollout" to a "change leadership" model that prioritizes human capability as the ultimate competitive advantage.

An interesting angle on the evolution of the modern workforce—and a fact people often get wrong—is that AI's primary impact isn't necessarily **job replacement**, but the **radical reshaping of roles** and the creation of a "new runtime" for how business operates.

The Common Misconception: AI as a Direct Human Replacement

Many people fear that AI is a "worker" coming to take their specific seat. However, research suggests that AI is more likely to reshape more jobs than it replaces.

- **The Jevons Paradox of Labor**: One counterintuitive fact is that as AI makes a task (like writing software) cheaper and faster, the total demand for that output can actually increase. For example, even as AI productivity for individual engineers rises, overall software engineering headcount has continued to grow because organizations now want to build more products than were previously affordable.
- **The Shift from "Doing" to "Managing"**: A critical fact people get wrong is thinking their current skills are "gold" when they are actually more like "milk"—they expire quickly. To stay relevant, workers must transition from

being the "worker" who produces answers to the "judge" or "system planner" who manages the machine's output.

The "Super Interesting" Angle: IA vs. AI

A compelling way to view this shift is the distinction between **AI (Artificial Intelligence)** and **IA (Intelligence Augmentation)**.

- **Intelligence Augmentation (IA)**: This perspective focuses on technology designed to *assist* human intelligence rather than replace it. The "interesting angle" here is that your job is likely safe if you focus on IA—using tools to extend your own capabilities.
- **Human-In-The-Loop (HITL)**: This model emphasizes a symbiotic relationship where AI handles repeatable, operational tasks (like routing calls), while humans focus on "edge cases" that require judgment and empathy.
- **The 68.7% Advantage**: Teams that combine AI and humans have been found to be **68.7% more effective** than either AI or humans working alone.

The Structural Reality: Traditional vs. AI-Centric Firms

In the book *Competing in the Age of AI*, the authors argue that the real "collision" isn't between humans and robots, but between **traditional firms** and **AI-centric firms**.

- **Structural Difference**: A traditional firm like Walmart is a retail company *using* AI, whereas Amazon is an AI company that *happens to sell retail*. The former is designed around human management hierarchies, while the latter is architected so that algorithms and data flow drive the entire organization.
- **The Leadership Priority**: Because of this, "upskilling"

isn't just a HR task; it is a fundamental leadership priority. The challenge for the modern workforce is not just learning to use a tool, but adapting to a world where the "product evolves faster than the strategy".

Introduction

The End of Traditional Limits

The Invisible Ceiling

For as long as there have been organizations, there have been limits. Limits of geography: a factory could only serve customers within a day's travel. Limits of capacity: a bank could only underwrite as many loans as its loan officers could process. Limits of information: a retailer could only stock what its buyers knew to order. Limits of coordination: a firm could only grow until the complexity of managing its own people consumed the value of serving its customers.

These limits were not bugs. They were features of the industrial operating model. They defined the possible. Every CEO, every strategist, every entrepreneur internalized them. To grow, you hired more people. To hire more people, you added more managers. To add more managers, you built more hierarchy. And at some point—different for every organization, but inevitable for all—the cost of adding one more person exceeded the value that person could produce. The firm hit its ceiling.

For two centuries, leaders accepted these ceilings as natural law. The only question was how close to the ceiling you could operate. The best firms—the Walmarts, the Goldmans, the McKinseys—pushed the ceiling higher through brilliant management, innovative processes, and relentless efficiency. But they never broke through. The ceiling was always there.

This book is about what happens when the ceiling disappears.

The Inversion

We are living through the most profound transformation in the economics of the firm since the invention of the factory. Artificial intelligence is not just another tool that organizations use. It is the new operating system upon which organizations run. It inverts every assumption of the industrial model.

In the old world, scale required headcount. Every additional customer required additional human attention. Every additional product required additional human coordination. The relationship was linear and inexorable.

In the new world, scale decouples from headcount. Algorithms serve millions of customers with the same infrastructure. Models improve with every transaction, reducing the need for human intervention. The marginal cost of serving one more customer approaches zero. The marginal cost of learning from that customer is negative: every transaction makes the system smarter.

This inversion is not theoretical. It is happening now. Ant Financial serves a billion customers with 10,000 employees. Traditional banks serve the same number with 200,000. Amazon adds billions in revenue each year while growing headcount at a fraction of that rate. Walmart—still a marvel of industrial efficiency—cannot match Amazon's velocity because it is playing a different game with different rules.

The old game was about optimizing human labor. The new game is about orchestrating algorithmic intelligence.

Why This Book Now

There is no shortage of books about AI. There are technical books about machine learning. There are business books about digital transformation. There are futurist books about the singularity. This book is none of those.

This book is about **organizational design in the age of AI**. It is for leaders who understand that AI is not a feature to be added to an existing organization but a new foundation upon which organizations must be rebuilt. It is for executives who sense that their operating models—designed for a world of scarce information and expensive coordination—are breaking down. It is for entrepreneurs who want to build the next generation of firms from first principles.

The book is organized around a single thesis: **The AI Factory is the new operating model of the firm.** The chapters that follow unpack what that means: how the factory works, what it enables, how it disrupts existing industries, how it transforms work, and how leaders must adapt.

Who This Book Is For

This book is written for three audiences.

First, **senior executives** in traditional organizations. You know your industry is changing. You see digital natives entering your market and taking share. You have launched AI pilots, maybe even scaled some. But you suspect that piecemeal efforts are not enough—that something fundamental about your organization needs to change. This book provides the framework for that change.

Second, **leaders of AI-native firms**. You have built your company around algorithms from the start. You understand the power of the virtuous data cycle. But as you scale, you face new challenges: managing hybrid human-machine teams, navigating ethical governance, sustaining innovation as you grow. This book helps you anticipate and address those challenges.

Third, **students and scholars** of strategy, organizations, and technology. You are studying the most important transformation in business since the Industrial Revolution. This book offers a conceptual framework—grounded in examples but aimed at principles—that will serve you as you analyze the firms of today and imagine the firms of tomorrow.

What You Will Learn

Each chapter builds on the last, creating a complete picture of the AI-centric firm.

Chapters 1-2 establish the foundation. Chapter 1 introduces the concept of the AI Factory as the new "runtime" of business, inverting the traditional relationship between growth and complexity. Chapter 2 dives inside the AI Factory, describing its four components and the shift from ad-hoc projects to platform-centric architecture.

Chapters 3-5 build the factory's internal capabilities. Chapter 3 covers the data pipeline—the lifeblood of intelligence. Chapter 4 explains the three algorithmic paradigms: supervised, unsupervised, and reinforcement learning. Chapter 5 describes the experimentation platform that moves the firm from correlation to causation.

Chapters 6-8 connect the factory to the outside world. Chapter 6 covers the digital backbone of APIs and cloud computing. Chapter 7 explains the virtuous data cycle of network and learning effects that creates winner-take-most dynamics. Chapter 8 describes strategic collisions between digital natives and analog incumbents.

Chapters 9-10 address the human dimension. Chapter 9 introduces the four categories of work: amplified, rebalanced, enabled, and vulnerable. Chapter 10 explores human-machine synthesis, focusing on judgment-intensive handoffs and workflow orchestration.

Chapters 11-12 conclude with leadership and ethics. Chapter 11 outlines the leadership mandate: strategic upskilling, operating model redesign, and organizational resilience. Chapter 12 addresses the ethical foundation: bias mitigation, responsible AI principles, and the new social contract for AI.

A Note on Examples

This book draws examples from a range of industries: retail (Amazon, Walmart), finance (Ant Financial, traditional banks), transportation (Tesla, Uber), technology (Google, Microsoft, Netflix), and others. These examples are illustrative, not exhaustive. The principles apply across sectors, from healthcare to logistics to media to professional services.

Where specific companies are mentioned, the goal is not to predict their futures or endorse their practices. It is to ground abstract concepts in concrete reality. The firms that dominate today may not dominate tomorrow. But the patterns they have revealed—the architectures, the dynamics, the trade-offs—will persist.

The Urgency

There is a temptation to read a book like this as a forecast of a distant future. The pace of change feels abstract until it arrives. The inevitability of disruption feels hypothetical until it is your industry, your company, your job.

The ceiling is not disappearing tomorrow. It is disappearing now. Every day, the AI Factory becomes more capable. Every day, the gap widens between organizations built for the old world and those built for the new. Every day, the cost of waiting grows.

This book is not a prediction. It is a manual. The factory is being built. The question is not whether it will transform your industry, but whether you will help build it—or be displaced by those who do.

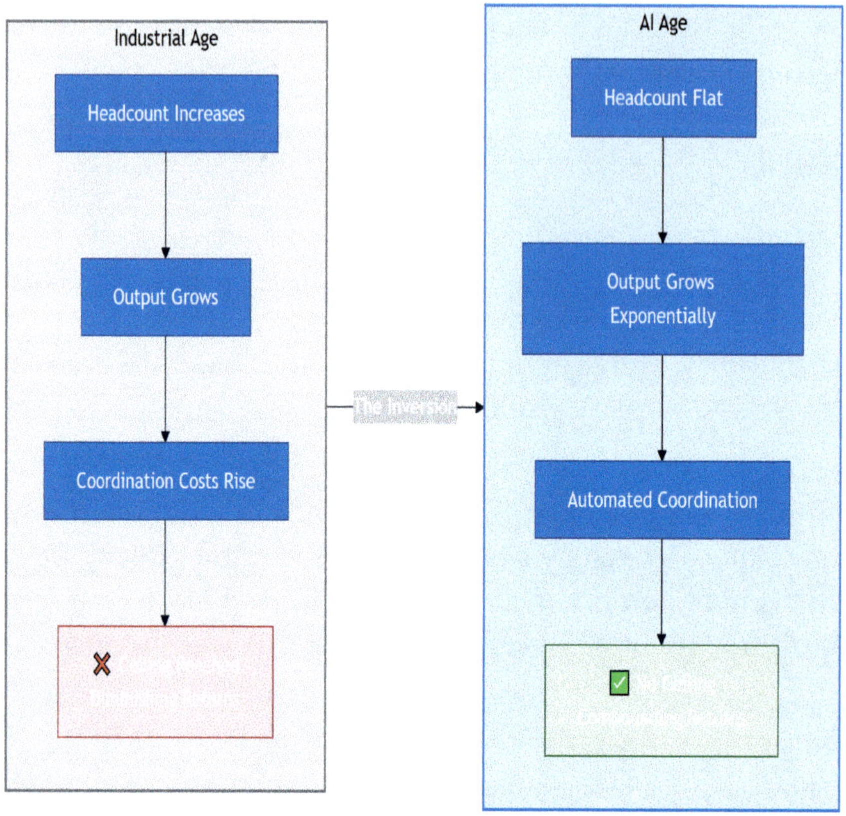
Industrial Age
Headcount Increases
Output Grows
Coordination Costs Rise
AI Age
Headcount Flat
Output Grows Exponentially
Automated Coordination
The Inversion

Chapter 1

The Age of AI New Operating Meta

The Pendulum of Industrial Progress

In the 1880s, a railroad executive faced a problem that had no precedent in human history. He commanded thousands of workers spread across thousands of miles of track, coordinating the movement of goods, labor, and capital across time zones that did not yet exist. His challenge was not mechanical—steam engines were reliable enough—but organizational. How do you ensure that a brakeman in Nebraska and a stationmaster in Pennsylvania act on the same information, follow the same rules, and make decisions that serve a single enterprise?

The answer, born over the next century, became the dominant operating meta of the industrial age: **standardize, delegate, and scale through hierarchy**. Firms increased productivity by breaking manual tasks into discrete steps, assigning each to a specialized role, and layering managers above managers to coordinate the whole. This model worked brilliantly—until it didn't. The very complexity that enabled scale eventually became its ceiling. Every new hire added not just productive capacity but also coordination overhead. Every new layer of management reduced the fidelity of information flowing upward and the speed of decisions flowing downward. Economists call this the complexity tax: the diminishing returns that set in when human coordination becomes the bottleneck.

For two centuries, the assumption was ironclad: **to grow output, you must grow headcount; to grow headcount, you must grow overhead**. The organization was a linear machine.

The Inversion

In the age of artificial intelligence, that assumption inverts.

Consider two companies. Company A, a regional bank, employs 200 loan officers who manually review credit applications. To double its loan volume, it must hire and train 200 more officers, plus additional managers and compliance staff. Company B, an AI-native lender, routes every application through a decision engine trained on decades of repayment data. Its loan volume can increase tenfold with the same engineering team and negligible marginal cost per decision.

The difference is not efficiency. It is architecture.

Company A is built around a human runtime: the execution of work flows through people, their schedules, their judgment calls, and their need for coordination. Company B is built around an algorithmic runtime: work flows through software, data pipelines, and automated decision boundaries. In Company A, intelligence is a scarce resource deployed manually. In Company B, intelligence is the operational foundation—ubiquitous, instantaneous, and parallelizable.

This is the core thesis of this book: **AI is not a tool that organizations use. It is the operating meta within which they now run.**

The New Runtime of Business

In software engineering, the runtime is the environment that executes a program's instructions. For most of corporate history, the runtime of business was human management. Strategy was translated into tasks, tasks were assigned to people, and people reported to other people. Every decision, from inventory replenishment to customer segmentation to pricing, required a human in the critical path.

AI changes which runtime governs. When a supply chain algorithm predicts demand and automatically places orders, the human has moved from decision-maker to supervisor—or, in many cases, has been removed entirely. When a personalization engine serves millions of unique product feeds simultaneously, no manager could have coordinated that complexity. The runtime has shifted.

The implications are radical and counterintuitive. Organizations that embrace AI as their core runtime exhibit a new property: **decoupling of growth from complexity**. They can scale output without scaling overhead. They can add new products, new markets, and new customers without adding proportionate coordination cost. The complexity tax is not eliminated—algorithms have their own failure modes—but it is fundamentally different in kind. Algorithmic systems do not tire, do not politic, and do not require alignment meetings. They scale horizontally across data and vertically across decision frequency.

What tasks are migrating from human to algorithmic runtime? A partial list from contemporary practice:

- Credit scoring and fraud detection

- Dynamic pricing and promotional optimization
- Inventory replenishment and supply chain routing
- Customer personalization and recommendation
- Hiring screening and resume filtering
- Quality inspection in manufacturing
- Claims processing in insurance

Each of these tasks once required teams of human specialists, supervised by managers, coordinated by analysts. Each now runs, in leading organizations, as automated pipelines executing thousands or millions of times per day.

The Four Pillars of the Intelligent Firm

If the runtime has changed, so must the architecture of the firm. This book is organized around four interdependent dimensions of the AI-centric enterprise.

Pillar One: The AI Factory

The AI Factory is the scalable decision engine that replaces traditional workflows. It is not a single technology but a system of systems: data ingestion pipelines, feature stores, model training infrastructure, deployment platforms, and continuous monitoring. The factory takes in raw data—customer behavior, sensor readings, transaction logs—and produces decisions: approve or deny, price high or low, stock or delay. The factory's currency is prediction, and its constraint is latency. Traditional workflows were measured in hours or days; the AI Factory operates in milliseconds or seconds.

Crucially, the AI Factory does not simply automate existing processes. It rearchitects them. A traditional call center routes customers to agents based on skills and availability. An AI Factory might predict the customer's intent from their first utterance, retrieve relevant information from internal systems, generate a response, and only escalate to a human when confidence falls below a threshold. The process is not faster—it is different.

Pillar Two: Strategic Impact

External markets respond to the AI Factory through two reinforcing mechanisms. First, **data network loops**: more customers generate more data, which improves the models, which attracts more customers. Second, **learning effects**: each decision the AI makes (and each outcome it observes) becomes a training signal for future decisions. Unlike human learning, which is slow and difficult to transfer, algorithmic learning is automatic and instantaneous across the entire system.

Together, these effects create winner-take-most dynamics. The AI-native firm does not just compete on price or quality; it competes on rate of improvement. A lagging firm cannot catch up simply by hiring better managers or running more meetings. It would need to match the data volume, the engineering talent, and the cumulative learning of the leader—a gap that widens over time.

Pillar Three: Workforce Transformation

If the AI Factory executes decisions and the strategic loops amplify advantage, what becomes of human work? The answer is not mass unemployment but redefinition. We identify three emerging categories:

- **Amplified roles**: Professionals whose core judgment is augmented by AI. A radiologist who reviews AI-generated annotations; an investment analyst who tests hypotheses against model outputs. Their productivity rises, but their function remains recognizable.
- **Rebalanced roles**: Positions where the distribution of tasks shifts dramatically. A customer service agent who spends 80% of time on complex problem-solving and 20% on routine inquiries (reversed from the pre-AI ratio). A software developer who writes specifications and reviews code but delegates implementation to AI pair programmers.
- **Enabled roles**: New categories that did not exist before AI. Prompt engineers, model behavior auditors, training data curators, fairness analysts. These roles require hybrid skills—technical fluency without necessarily full-stack engineering—and are often the fastest-growing segments of AI-centric firms.

Then there is the **vulnerable** category: roles defined by routine, repetitive decisions with clear pattern-matching. Telemarketing, basic data entry, simple document review, conventional loan underwriting. These roles are not necessarily eliminated but become algorithmically compressible—their economic value collapses as AI performs them at near-zero marginal cost. The management of vulnerable labor is both a humanitarian obligation and a strategic risk, as we explore in later chapters.

Pillar Four: The Leadership Mandate

None of the above happens automatically. The leadership mandate is twofold: technical and moral.

Technically, leaders must orchestrate the transition from human runtime to algorithmic runtime. This requires investment in data infrastructure (often unglamorous), recruiting of hybrid talent (engineers who understand business, managers who understand statistics), and redesign of processes that have remained unchanged for decades. The single most common failure mode is pilot paralysis—hundreds of small AI experiments that never reach production because no one has authority over the shared runtime.

Morally, leaders must govern what algorithms optimize. An AI Factory trained on historical data will reproduce historical biases. A learning loop that maximizes short-term engagement may optimize for outrage or addiction. A pricing algorithm with no fairness constraints may discover illegal collusion. The leadership mandate is not to reject AI for these risks but to design governance systems—monitoring, redress, continuous audit—that match the speed and scale of the runtime itself.

"Doing" AI vs. "Being" AI

The most consequential distinction in this book is between two postures an organization can adopt.

Doing AI means treating AI as a set of features to be retrofit into an existing organizational structure. The hierarchy remains; the reporting lines remain; the coordination through meetings and email remains. AI is added like a new machine on a factory floor —useful, perhaps transformative in parts, but subordinate to the human runtime. Walmart, for all its investment in machine learning for inventory and personalization, remains structurally a retail company that uses AI. Its critical path still runs through regional managers, store associates, and human-led supply chain reviews.

Being AI means building the organization around the algorithmic runtime from first principles. The hierarchy is flat or entirely absent. Coordination happens through shared data models and APIs, not through managers. Decisions default to automation, with human overrides as the exception. Amazon is not a retail company that uses AI. It is an AI company that happens to sell retail. Its flywheel—search, recommendation, fulfillment optimization, dynamic pricing—is a single integrated algorithmic system. The same is true of Google (advertising as an AI system), Uber (dispatch as an AI system), and a growing number of insurgents in finance, logistics, and healthcare.

The implications of this distinction are profound. A doing-AI firm can improve incrementally. A being-AI firm can grow exponentially. A doing-AI firm enters new markets by acquisition and integration. A being-AI firm enters new markets by extending its algorithmic runtime—which takes days or weeks, not months or years. A doing-AI firm has a cost structure that is linear in revenue. A being-AI firm has a cost structure that is sublinear—and sometimes near-zero at the margin.

This is why the first dramatic implications of artificial intelligence are not the simulation of human consciousness. They are not artificial general intelligence, not the singularity, not the alignment problem as usually debated. The first dramatic implications are organizational: who can build what, how fast, and at what cost. The firms that understand this will reshape industries before incumbents realize the rules have changed.

Caption: The operating meta of business has shifted from human coordination to algorithmic execution.

A side-by-side comparison of two organizational architectures.

Dimension	Traditional Firm (Human Runtime)	AI-Centric Firm (Algorithmic Runtime)
Critical Path	Human managers, intuition, and meetings	Software, data pipelines, and the AI Factory
Scaling	Linear: Increasing output requires a proportional increase in headcount.	Sublinear: Output grows exponentially while headcount remains relatively flat.
Coordination	Silos, hierarchy, and strict reporting lines.	APIs, shared data models, and network-based integration.
Learning Speed	Periodic/Batched: Quarterly reviews and manual analysis.	Continuous: Learning occurs in real-time with every transaction.
Marginal Cost	Positive and constant (every new unit has a set cost).	Approaches Zero: Digital distribution and automation collapse unit costs.

Figure 1: The Shift from Human Runtime to Algorithmic Runtime

Key Insight: The Diminishing Returns Barrier

In a traditional firm, growth eventually hits a ceiling of complexity. Managing more people and more assets creates "friction" that slows down decision-making.

In contrast, the **AI-Centric Firm** replaces human bottlenecks with a digital core. This allows the organization to bypass traditional scale constraints. As the diagram below would illustrate, while a traditional company's costs grow alongside its revenue, an AI-driven company sees its cost curve flatten while its value creation accelerates due to network and learning effects.

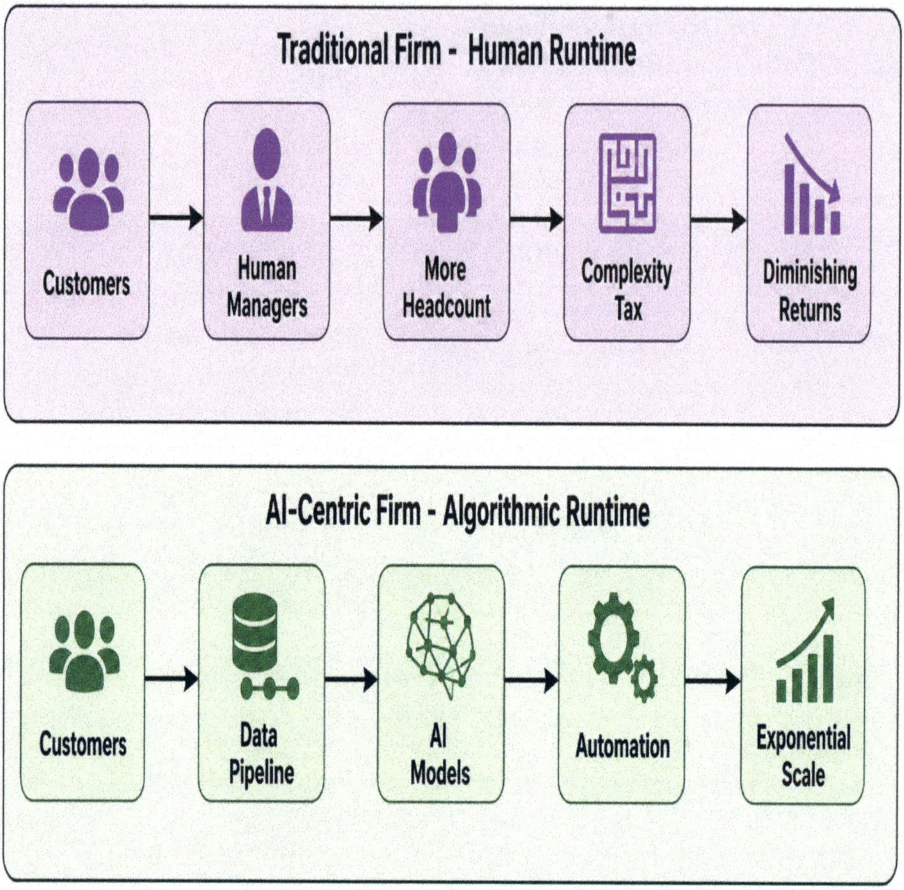

The New Meta: Leadership and Strategy in the Age of AI

The Foundational Shift: From Product to System

The emergence of artificial intelligence is not merely a technological wave but a fundamental transformation of the firm itself. Traditional companies historically competed by building better products, but in the modern era, success is defined by building better **systems**. While humans traditionally designed and executed operational systems, AI has become the "runtime" of the firm—the core engine that shapes the execution of all tasks in real time. This shift moves software instructions and algorithms into the **critical path** of value delivery, allowing firms to achieve levels of scale, scope, and learning that were previously constrained by human limitations.

The Architecture of the AI Factory

At the heart of this new breed of firm is the **AI Factory**, a scalable decision engine that treats decision-making as an industrial process. The factory consists of four essential components:

1. **The Data Pipeline:** A systematic process to gather, clean, and safeguard data, which serves as the "fuel" for the system.
2. **Algorithm Development:** The "machines" that generate predictions about future business states.
3. **Experimentation Platform:** A mechanism to test hypotheses (such as A/B testing) to ensure changes have the intended causal effect.
4. **Software Infrastructure:** The "pipes" that embed these processes in a consistent computing environment.

This system creates a **virtuous cycle**: more usage leads to more data, which leads to better algorithms and services, further increasing usage. Unlike traditional firms that face diminishing returns as they grow, AI-driven models can experience **increasing returns to scale**, as their marginal cost of serving an additional user is virtually zero.

Intelligence Augmentation (IA): Reckoning vs. Judgment

A successful transition to this new era requires mastering **Intelligence Augmentation (IA)**—the partnership where humans and AI accomplish more together than either could alone. This collaboration is built on the distinction between two modes of operation:

- **Reckoning (AI):** Calculative prediction grounded in facts and historical data. AI excels at structured, predictable tasks like routing calls or identifying spreadsheet duplicates.
- **Judgment (Human):** Practical wisdom informed by lived experience, empathy, and ethical considerations. Humans understand the "why" behind a job—factors AI cannot know.

The goal of this partnership is **workflow orchestration**: identifying the "trigger points" where the AI stops and the human takes over. When AI handles routine "reckoning" and humans focus on "judgment-intensive" edge cases, teams can become nearly **69% (68.7%) more effective** than either working in isolation.

Strategic Collisions and Industry Reshaping

When firms with digital operating models enter traditional markets, a **strategic collision** occurs. Because digital firms aggregate data and leverage network effects, they can rapidly overwhelm incumbents. For example, in just over a decade, **Airbnb** scaled to offer three times the lodging capacity that **Marriott** accumulated in a century. Similarly, **Nokia's** product-focused model, despite its engineering excellence, was crushed by the platform-focused ecosystems of **Apple's iOS** and **Google's Android** because Nokia lacked a consistent digital foundation for developers.

In this new landscape, competitive advantage shifts from specialized vertical expertise to **universal horizontal capabilities** in data sourcing and algorithm development. Industries are disappearing as clear boundaries give way to **recombination**, where firms like **Amazon** or **Alibaba** use their data hubs to bridge into entirely different sectors like healthcare or banking.

The Human Cost: Anxiety, Burnout, and Ethics

The speed of AI transformation is currently outpacing organizational trust. Nearly **7 in 10 US employees (69%)** fear AI will lead to layoffs within three years, and **49%** fear losing their own jobs. This job insecurity, combined with an "always-on" work culture, has led to rising burnout, with **51% of workers** reporting they have cried because of work stress in the past month.

Furthermore, digital operating models introduce severe ethical risks:

- **Digital Amplification:** Algorithms designed for engagement can inadvertently weaponize misinformation, such as anti-vaccination propaganda.
- **Algorithmic Bias:** Systems can mirror and amplify human prejudices, such as facial recognition software that is less accurate for women of color or recruitment tools that penalize female candidates.
- **Cybersecurity:** The concentration of massive datasets creates "nightmare scenarios" for breaches, as seen in the **Equifax** hack affecting 147.9 million people.

Future-Proofing: Becoming a System Planner

To remain relevant, professionals must shift from being **"Task-Doers"** to **"System Planners"**. In the "Agility Era," the half-life of technical skills is now closer to **2.5 years**; if you are doing work the same way you did 18 months ago, you are becoming outdated.

Durable career success relies on **metacognition**—thinking about how you think. Professionals must embrace three rules for the new meta:

1. **The Flow Rule:** Constantly shed old habits and tools to make room for new ones.

2. **The Question Finder:** Focus on asking the right questions and framing problems, as facts are now "cheap" and ubiquitous.
3. **The Strategy Check:** Move up the chain from executing work to being the "checker" who validates the machine's logic and gives the final okay.

Ultimately, the leaders who thrive will be those who view AI not as a feature to be installed, but as a foundation to be architected with wisdom, responsibility, and constant adaptation

What does a scalable AI factory look like in practice?

A scalable **AI factory** is the operational core of a modern digital firm, functioning as a decision-making engine that treats data analysis as an industrial process. Unlike traditional models where humans make individual choices, the AI factory systematically converts data into **predictions and automated actions** that drive task execution in real time.

In practice, a scalable AI factory consists of four essential components and operates through a "virtuous cycle" of improvement.

1. The Four Essential Components

- **The Data Pipeline:** This is the "fuel" of the factory. It systematically gathers, cleans, normalizes, and safeguards data to ensure it is accurate and usable. For example, **Netflix** gathers billions of ratings and millions of "stream plays" daily, tracking when viewers pause or skip content to create a granular "datafied" view of entertainment.

- **Algorithm Development:** Algorithms act as the "machines" that generate predictions about future business states. These include **supervised learning** (recognizing known patterns), **unsupervised learning** (discovering new insights), and **reinforcement learning** (optimizing decisions through trial and error).
- **Experimentation Platform:** This component tests hypotheses—such as A/B testing—to ensure that new algorithms have a **causal effect** on business outcomes before they are fully deployed. **Google** and **LinkedIn** run tens of thousands of such experiments annually to validate data-driven improvements.
- **Software Infrastructure:** These are the "pipes" that embed the data and algorithms into a consistent, componentized computing environment. This infrastructure is increasingly cloud-based and uses **APIs** (Application Programming Interfaces) to allow different teams to "subscribe" to clean data and build new applications in days rather than months.

2. The Virtuous Cycle of Scale

A scalable factory creates a self-reinforcing loop: **more usage** leads to **more data**, which trains **better algorithms**, resulting in a **better service**, which then attracts even more usage.

- **Example (Ant Financial):** Its MYbank uses a "**3-1-0**" system: 3 minutes to apply for a loan, 1 second for AI to approve it, and 0 human interaction. Every loan issued generates more data, making the next credit decision more accurate.
- **Example (Ocado):** AI predicts customer grocery needs days in advance and runs thousands of routing calculations per second to optimize its fleet, allowing the business to scale without the typical complexity costs of a human-managed warehouse.

3. Removing the Human Bottleneck

A key practical feature of a scalable factory is moving human labor off the **"critical path"** of value delivery.

- **Designers vs. Doers:** Employees stop performing routine tasks (like approving individual loans or setting daily prices) and instead become **designers and overseers** of the digital systems that do the work.
- **Zero Marginal Cost:** Because the "runtime" is software-driven, the cost of serving an additional user is virtually zero. This allows firms like **Airbnb** to offer three times the lodging capacity of Marriott with a fraction of the employees.

4. Practical Implementation: The Bezos Mandate

To make a factory scalable, the organization must be **modular**. At **Amazon**, Jeff Bezos famously mandated that all teams expose their data and functionality through service interfaces (APIs). This architectural shift broke down traditional organizational silos, ensuring that data could flow freely into the AI factory rather than being trapped in disconnected departments.

The Result: Superior Performance

Research on over 350 enterprises shows that "AI maturity leaders"—those with fully functional AI factories—enjoy significantly higher financial returns. These leaders saw an average **gross margin of 55%**, compared to just **37% for laggards** who still relied on siloed, manual processes

Can you explain the 'virtuous cycle' of scale for algorithms?

The **"virtuous cycle"** of scale for algorithms is a self-reinforcing loop at the core of an **AI factory** that systematically converts user engagement into improved performance and increased business value. Unlike traditional businesses that often face diminishing returns as they grow, this cycle allows digital firms to achieve **increasing returns to scale**.

The cycle consists of four interconnected stages:

1. Increased Usage and Engagement

The process begins when users interact with a digital service, such as performing a search, watching a video, or applying for a loan. Every interaction serves as a touchpoint that triggers the system.

2. Data Collection

More usage leads to the accumulation of **more data**. This data includes not just explicit actions (like a purchase) but also granular behavioural points, such as when a user pauses a video, mouse-overs an image, or types specific letters into a search box.

3. Algorithm Refinement

This incoming data is used to **refine and train algorithms**. Because AI and machine learning thrive on data, the more information they process, the more accurate their predictions become. Essentially, the more the system operates, the **"smarter"** it gets—a phenomenon described as the "network effect applied to intelligence".

4. Better Service and Value

As algorithms improve, the service becomes more effective, providing better recommendations, more accurate pricing, or more personalized experiences. This **better service** creates exceptional consumer value, which in turn attracts **more usage**, restarting the cycle.

Practical Examples of the Cycle

- **Search Engines:** When a user types into a search box, algorithms predict the term based on past data. Every click or "move away" from a result provides a data point that improves predictions for the next search.

- **Ant Financial:** Every loan issued by the "3-1-0" system generates data that makes the next creditworthiness decision faster and more accurate.
- **Netflix:** The system monitors viewing habits to determine which movie thumbnails to show. If a user clicks on a specific image, that data point reinforces the algorithm's understanding of that user's "taste community".

By removing human labor from the **critical path** of these loops, the AI factory ensures that the system does not decrease in efficiency as it grows. Instead, the more data the system gathers through scale, the more the value curve ratchets upward

What are the four essential components of an AI factory?

An **AI factory** is the scalable decision engine that powers the digital operating model of a modern firm. It systematically converts data into predictions, insights, and choices that guide or automate operational actions.

According to the sources, the four essential components of an AI factory are:

- **1. Data Pipeline:** This is the systematic process of gathering, cleaning, normalizing, and safeguarding data. Because data is the "fuel" of the factory, this pipeline must be sustainable and scalable, ensuring the information is accurate and integrated across the enterprise before it is used for analysis.

- **2. Algorithm Development:** These algorithms are the "machines" that generate predictions about future states or actions of the business. They are the "beating heart" of the digital firm and typically utilize machine learning approaches such as supervised, unsupervised, or reinforcement learning to drive critical operating activities.
- **3. Experimentation Platform:** This is the mechanism used to test hypotheses regarding new prediction and decision algorithms. It ensures that suggested changes are actually having the intended **causal effect** on business outcomes through methods like A/B testing before they are fully deployed into production.
- **4. Software Infrastructure:** These systems embed the data pipeline and algorithms into a consistent, componentized computing environment. This infrastructure—increasingly cloud-based—uses tools like APIs to connect the factory's outputs to both internal and external users, allowing for the rapid deployment of new AI applications.

Together, these components create a **"virtuous cycle"**: more usage leads to more data, which trains better algorithms, resulting in a better service that attracts even more usage. This industrialised approach to decision-making allows digital firms to achieve levels of scale, scope, and learning that traditional human-centric models cannot match

What does software infrastructure provide in an AI company?

In an AI-driven company, software infrastructure serves as the essential framework that embeds and integrates all other components of the **AI factory**—the data pipeline, algorithms, and experimentation platform—into a consistent operating environment.

According to the sources, software infrastructure provides the following critical functions:

1. The "Pipes" for Data Delivery

If data is considered the "fuel" of an AI company, the software infrastructure constitutes the **"pipes"** that deliver that fuel to the "machines" (the algorithms). It ensures that processed data is moved systematically from its source through the pipeline and into the applications where it can be used for predictions and decision-making.

2. A Componentized Platform for Rapid Development

State-of-the-art infrastructure provides a modular structure—often a **data platform**—that allows developers to build, deploy, and execute AI applications quickly.

- **APIs (Application Programming Interfaces):** Infrastructure uses a "publish-subscribe" methodology for APIs, making clean and consistent data available like a "data supermarket".
- **Building Blocks:** This allows agile teams to use common software building blocks to create new applications in weeks or even days, rather than months.
- **Modularity:** It enables different teams to work independently on specific use cases without disrupting the consistency of the entire system.

3. Connectivity and Accessibility

The infrastructure connects the factory's outputs to both **internal and external users**. It bridges the gap between the core digital processes (like Netflix's recommendation engine or Amazon's pricing systems) and the end-user experience. It also manages how data is exposed to external partners and third-party developers through secure APIs.

4. Scalable and Robust Computing Power

Modern software infrastructure is increasingly **cloud-based**, which provides several advantages:

- **Scalability on Demand:** It allows companies to add computing and storage capacity as they grow without running into traditional physical constraints.

- **Standardization:** It often utilizes standard off-the-shelf components and open-source software, making it easier to maintain and update.
- **Security and Governance:** It provides a centralized location for safeguarding sensitive data and enforcing consistent security policies.

Summary Table: The Role of Infrastructure

Feature	Functional Benefit
Embedding	Integrates data pipelines, algorithms, and experiments into one system.
API Structures	Provides "supermarket-style" access to clean data for developers.
Connectivity	Links the AI factory to users, partners, and external applications.
Cloud-Based	Ensures the system is robust, secure, and infinitely scalable.

Figure 1.1: The Shift from Human Runtime to Algorithmic Runtime

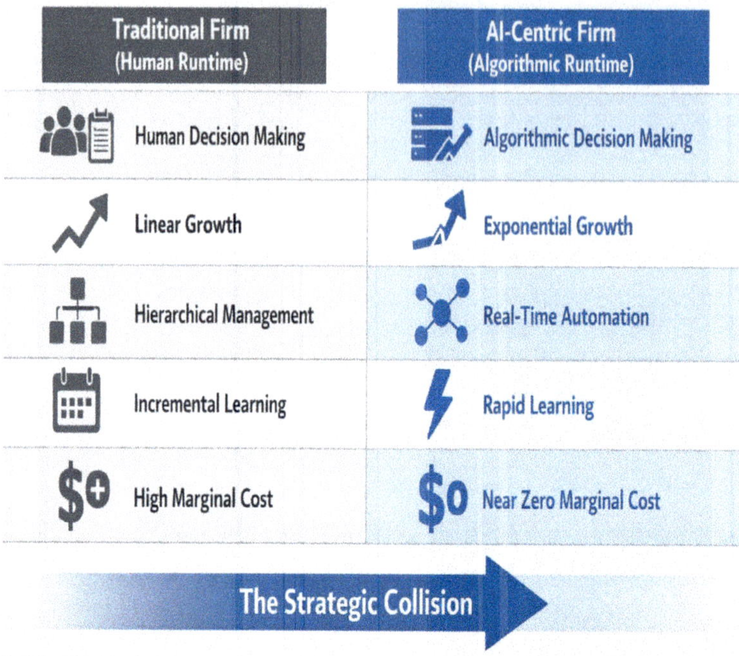

Chapter 2

The AI Factory Core:Designing the Scalable Decision Engine

The Industrialization of Intelligence

In Chapter 1, we introduced the central inversion of the AI age: growth need no longer imply proportional complexity. The mechanism that makes this inversion possible is the **AI Factory**—the scalable decision engine that sits at the heart of every intelligent firm.

Consider Ant Financial, the financial affiliate of Alibaba. In 2020, Ant served over one billion customers and tens of millions of small businesses, processing loans, insurance claims, and investment allocations. Its workforce? Roughly 10,000 employees. Compare this to a traditional global bank like Bank of America, which serves a similar number of customers but employs over 200,000 people. The difference is not efficiency in the conventional sense. It is architecture.

Ant Financial is not a bank that uses AI. It is an AI Factory that happens to offer financial services. Every loan application, every fraud detection, every credit score update flows through automated pipelines. A small-business owner applying for a loan receives a decision in three minutes—not because Ant's employees work faster, but because no human touches the decision path at all.

The AI Factory industrializes intelligence. Where an industrial factory takes raw materials—steel, rubber, plastic—and transforms them into physical goods, the AI Factory takes raw data—transaction logs, sensor readings, customer clicks—and transforms it into actionable intelligence: predictions, classifications, recommendations, automations. This industrialization is what allows AI-centric firms to operate at a scale and speed that traditional organizations cannot match.

From Ad-Hoc Projects to Platform Architecture

Most organizations begin their AI journey with projects. A team in marketing builds a churn prediction model. A team in operations builds a demand forecasting model. A team in risk builds a fraud detection model. Each project is treated as a discrete initiative with its own budget, its own data pipeline, its own infrastructure. This is the ad-hoc project phase, and it is where the vast majority of firms remain stuck.

The problem with ad-hoc projects is not that they fail—many succeed. The problem is that they do not compound. Each project builds its own silo. Data is copied and transformed separately for each use case. Models are deployed on different schedules with different monitoring tools. Engineers solving data cleaning problems in marketing have no idea that operations just solved the same problem last quarter. The organization accumulates AI artifacts, not AI capability.

The transition to a mature AI organization is marked by a shift from **projects to platform**. The AI Factory is that platform: a shared, multi-layered architecture that any team can draw upon, and to which every new project contributes. When marketing builds a churn model, their work enriches the customer data feature store that operations can reuse. When operations builds a demand forecaster, their monitoring dashboards become templates for risk. The factory learns across projects, not just within them.

This is the difference between having AI and being an AI Factory. The former is a collection of experiments. The latter is an operating system.

The Three Layers of the AI Factory

The AI Factory is not a single piece of software but a stack of capabilities, each layer feeding the next.

Layer One: The Data Pipeline

Raw data is not a resource. It is a liability—until it is ingested, cleaned, structured, and made available. The data pipeline is the Factory's intake system. It handles:

•**Ingestion**: Streaming or batch collection from internal systems (transaction databases, CRM logs, sensor networks) and external sources (market feeds, social media APIs, partner data).
•**Cleaning**: Handling missing values, correcting inconsistencies, standardizing formats. This is unglamorous work, but more models fail because of dirty data than because of algorithm choice.
•**Feature engineering**: Transforming raw data into predictive signals. A timestamp becomes "hour of day," "day of week," "days since last purchase." A customer address becomes "distance to nearest distribution center." Feature engineering encodes human domain knowledge into machine-readable form.

•**Storage and access**: A feature store—a centralized repository where cleaned, versioned features are available for any model to consume.

Without a robust data pipeline, the rest of the factory cannot function. Yet this layer is chronically underinvested in, because it lacks the glamour of machine learning. Leaders who skip the pipeline build models on quicksand.

Layer Two: Algorithmic Processing

The assembly line of the AI Factory. Raw features enter; predictions and decisions exit. This layer includes:

•**Model training**: Algorithms learn patterns from historical data. Which algorithm? The answer is almost always less important than the quality and quantity of the data. A simple logistic regression on excellent features will outperform a deep neural network on noisy features.
•**Model deployment**: Trained models are pushed to production, where they serve predictions in real time or in batch. Deployment is where most projects die, because production environments have constraints—latency, throughput, memory—that development environments ignore.
•**Model serving**: The runtime execution of predictions. A credit scoring model receives an application and returns a risk score within 100 milliseconds. A recommendation model receives a user ID and returns a list of products.

Critically, algorithmic processing is parallelizable in a way human processing is not. A human loan officer reviews one file at a time. An AI Factory can process 100,000 applications simultaneously. This is not a speed advantage. It is a structural advantage.

Layer Three: Action and Feedback

The output of the AI Factory is not predictions for their own sake. It is action. A fraud prediction triggers a transaction block. A demand forecast triggers an inventory order. A personalization score triggers a webpage render.

But action is not the end of the factory's work. It is the beginning of a feedback loop. Every decision produces an outcome: the transaction was real or fraudulent, the inventory ordered was sufficient or insufficient, the recommended product was clicked or ignored. These outcomes become labels that feed back into the data pipeline, enabling retraining and continuous improvement.

This feedback loop is the source of the AI Factory's compounding advantage. Traditional organizations learn slowly, through quarterly reviews and post-mortems. The AI Factory learns continuously, with every prediction generating a training signal for the next.

The Platform-Centric Model vs. Siloed Experimentation

The table below captures the contrast between the immature and mature states of AI organization:

Dimension	Ad-Hoc Projects (Siloed)	AI Factory (Platform-Centric)
Data	Copied into each project; inconsistent definitions and duplication	Centralized feature store with a single source of truth
Infrastructure	Every team builds its own pipelines and deployment tools	Shared training, serving, and monitoring infrastructure
Models	One-off deployments with manual oversight	Continuous integration and deployment (CI/CD) for models with automated monitoring
Talent	Generalists responsible for the full stack	Specialized roles (data engineers, ML engineers, product managers, governance leads) working on a common platform
Output	Isolated insights and disconnected use cases	Compounding organizational capability that improves with each deployment
Failure Mode	Pilot paralysis—proofs of concept that never reach production	Success that scales so rapidly it strains downstream systems and governance

The most common failure mode in the left column is *pilot paralysis*: dozens of successful proofs-of-concept that never reach production because no team owns the path from notebook to live system. The most common failure mode in the right column is different: success that overwhelms the organization. A model that works too well can generate more volume than downstream systems can handle. A pricing algorithm that discovers an unexpected pattern can produce results that no human understands. Scaling the factory requires not just technical infrastructure but also governance

Removing Traditional Bottlenecks

The AI Factory removes two bottlenecks that have constrained organizations for centuries.

The bottleneck of human capacity. In a traditional firm, every decision requires a human in the loop. Humans have limited attention, work at fixed speeds, and cannot parallelize beyond trivial concurrency. The AI Factory replaces the human-in-the-loop with a model-in-the-loop for routine decisions, reserving human attention for exceptions, edge cases, and strategic judgment. The result is not automation for its own sake but capacity liberation: humans focus on problems that require creativity, empathy, or cross-contextual reasoning, while algorithms handle pattern recognition at scale.

The bottleneck of geography. Industrial firms located decisions where workers were located. A loan officer had to be in the same country as the applicant, both for regulatory reasons and because face-to-face interaction was assumed necessary. The AI Factory has no physical location. Ant Financial processes loan applications from rural farmers in China using the same infrastructure that processes applications from street vendors in Shanghai. The model does not commute. It does not take lunch. It does not require a local office. This decoupling of decision-making from geography enables firms to serve populations that traditional organizations found unprofitable or impossible to reach.

Strategic Adaptability in a Fluid Environment

Traditional organizational design assumes stable industry boundaries. A bank competes with other banks. A retailer competes with other retailers. The AI Factory operates under a different assumption: industry lines are dissolving.

Consider what happens when an AI Factory's core capability—real-time personalized recommendations—can be applied to movies (Netflix), to products (Amazon), to restaurants (DoorDash), and to jobs (LinkedIn). The underlying factory is the same. Only the input data and output actions change. This is **strategic adaptability**: the ability to enter adjacent markets not by acquiring new capabilities but by pointing existing ones at new problems.

For a traditional firm, entering a new market requires years of planning, hiring, and capital expenditure. For an AI-centric firm, entering a new market requires a data integration and a configuration change. When Amazon entered cloud computing (AWS), it did not build a new organization from scratch. It repurposed the infrastructure built for retail—the same data centers, the same scaling patterns, the same automation logic—and offered it as a service. Competitors could not follow quickly because they did not have the factory to repurpose.

This adaptability creates a new competitive dynamic. The threat to an incumbent is not always a direct competitor in the same industry. It is an AI Factory from an adjacent industry that discovers that its capabilities apply to the incumbent's problem. The hotel industry was not disrupted by a better hotel chain. It was disrupted by a software company (Airbnb) with a matching engine. The taxi industry was not disrupted by a better taxi company. It was disrupted by a logistics AI Factory (Uber) with real-time dispatch.

From Technical Oversight to Organizational Design

Most discussions of the AI Factory focus on technical choices: which database, which framework, which model architecture. These matter, but they are not the primary challenge. The primary challenge is organizational.

Building an AI Factory requires redesigning the firm around data flows rather than departmental silos. In a traditional organization, information moves vertically—up the chain of command and back down. In an AI Factory, information moves horizontally, through shared data pipelines and APIs. This inverts the logic of authority. A manager who controls access to information loses power when information is available to any system with the right credentials. A department that guarded its data as a proprietary asset loses leverage when the feature store centralizes everything.

This is why incumbents struggle to build AI Factories even when they hire the best talent and buy the best technology. The organizational immune system rejects the factory because the factory threatens existing power structures. Leaders who understand this do not focus solely on technology. They focus on re-architecting authority: changing who decides what, who sees what, and who is measured by what.

What the AI Factory Enables

When fully operational, the AI Factory enables three capabilities that are impossible in traditional organizations:

1. **Real-time execution at scale.** Decisions happen in milliseconds, not days. A fraud detection model evaluates a transaction before the customer removes their finger from the keypad. A pricing model updates offers while the customer browses.
2. **Continuous learning without friction.** Every interaction becomes a training example. The factory improves not despite its volume but because of it. Traditional organizations improve through scheduled reviews; the AI Factory improves through every transaction.
3. **Marginal cost approaching zero for routine decisions.** The thousandth loan application costs essentially the same as the first —the marginal cost is electricity and compute time, not human salary and benefits. This collapses the cost structure of any industry built on routine judgment.

The Path Ahead

This chapter has described the what of the AI Factory. Chapter 3 turns to the so what: how the factory creates strategic impact through data network loops and learning effects, and why these dynamics lead to winner-take-most markets. For now, the key insight is this: the AI Factory is not a technology project. It is the core engine of the intelligent firm. Organizations that build it well will scale without friction. Organizations that fail to build it will find themselves competing not against other firms but against the fundamental economics of the age.

The factory does not rest. Neither can they.

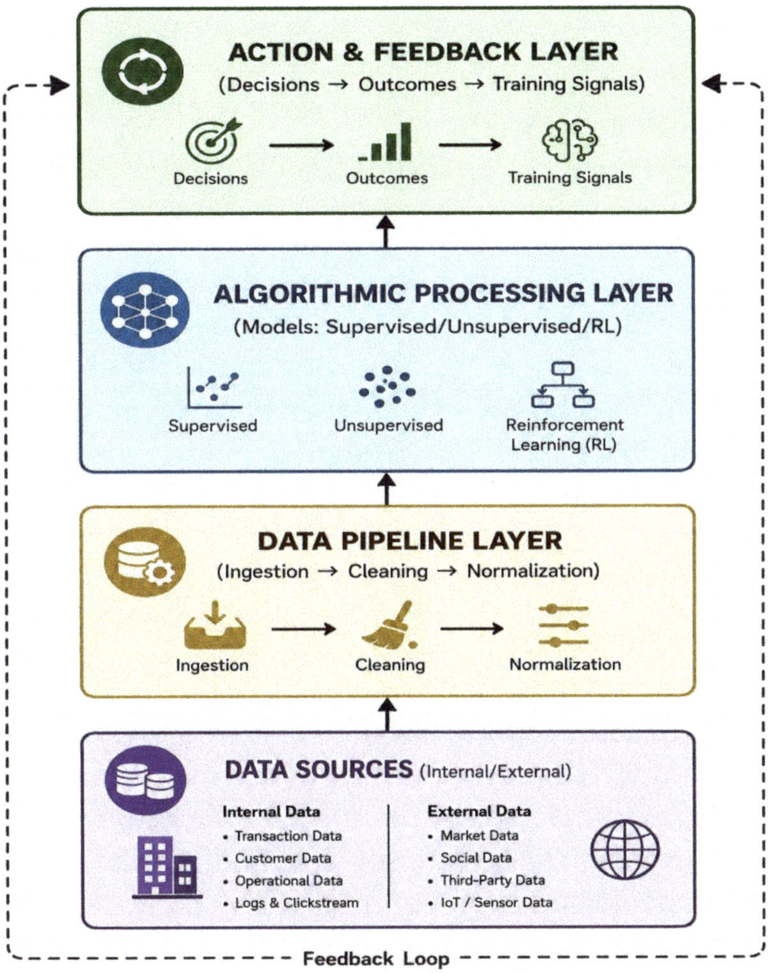

Figure 2: The AI Factory Architecture

Caption: The AI Factory transforms raw data into actionable intelligence through a closed-loop, multi-layer architecture.

Chapter 3

The Lifeblood of Intelligence: Navigating the Data Pipeline

The Hidden Failure Mode

In Chapter 2, we described the AI Factory as the scalable decision engine of the intelligent firm. We detailed its three layers: the data pipeline, algorithmic processing, and action with feedback. But we glossed over a critical fact: **the vast majority of AI projects fail before they ever reach the algorithmic layer.** They fail not because the models are poorly designed, but because the data is unusable.

Consider a cautionary tale from the financial sector. A regional bank spent eighteen months and twelve million dollars building a sophisticated fraud detection system. They hired PhDs in machine learning. They deployed the latest deep learning architectures. They achieved 99% accuracy in offline testing. When the system went live, it performed worse than the simple rule-based system it replaced. The reason? The training data had been carefully cleaned by a dedicated team before it reached the data scientists. The live data stream was full of inconsistencies, missing fields, and legacy codes that the training data never contained. The models had learned to detect fraud in a world that did not exist.

This is the hidden failure mode of AI. Leaders focus on algorithms because algorithms are exciting. They underinvest in data pipelines because pipelines are unglamorous. But a brilliant algorithm on bad data will always lose to a simple algorithm on excellent data. **Garbage in, garbage out** is not a cliché. It is the first law of the AI Factory.

What Is the Data Pipeline?

The data pipeline is the intake and preparation system of the AI Factory. It takes raw data from its sources—transaction logs, sensor readings, customer interactions, external APIs—and transforms it into a form that algorithms can consume. This transformation involves four distinct stages, each with its own failure modes.

Stage One: Ingestion

Raw data enters the pipeline from wherever it lives. Internal sources include application databases, server logs, CRM systems, and enterprise resource planning (ERP) tools. External sources include third-party APIs, public datasets, social media feeds, and partner data sharing agreements. Internet of Things (IoT) sensors add another dimension: millions of devices streaming telemetry in real time.

The challenge of ingestion is not technical but organizational. Data lives in silos. Sales uses Salesforce. Operations uses Oracle. Marketing uses HubSpot. Each system was purchased independently, managed by a different team, and optimized for a different purpose. Getting these systems to speak to each other requires not just API connections but political agreements: who owns the data, who can access it, who is responsible for its accuracy.

Effective ingestion does not wait for perfect integration. It starts with the 80% that is accessible and builds connectors incrementally. The alternative—waiting for a multi-year "data transformation program"—is almost always a path to failure.

Stage Two: Cleaning

Raw data is dirty. It contains missing values, duplicate records, inconsistent formatting, and outright errors. A customer's birthdate might be entered as "01/01/1900" when the true date is unknown. A product code might appear as "ABC-123" in one system and "ABC123" in another. A transaction timestamp might be in Eastern Time in one database and UTC in another.

Cleaning is the process of detecting and correcting these issues. It is manual, tedious, and endless. No organization ever finishes cleaning its data; it only reaches a state of being clean enough for the current use case.

The most important decision in cleaning is what to leave dirty. Perfectly clean data is a myth. The goal is systematic handling of known issues: missing values are imputed or flagged; duplicates are deduplicated according to rules; inconsistent formats are normalized. The organization that spends six months scrubbing every possible error before any model is built will be overtaken by the organization that builds a "good enough" pipeline and iterates.

Stage Three: Normalization

Different sources speak different languages. One system stores dates as "YYYY-MM-DD." Another stores them as "MM/DD/YYYY." One system measures distance in miles, another in kilometers. One system labels customers as "active/inactive," another as "1/0."

Normalization is the process of translating these disparate formats into a single, consistent schema. A customer is always identified by the same unique key across all systems. A timestamp always includes timezone information. A categorical variable always uses the same set of labels.

Normalization is where the data pipeline begins to create value beyond the immediate use case. A normalized data lake—or, more precisely, a feature store—becomes an organizational asset that multiple teams can draw upon. When marketing and operations and risk all use the same definition of "customer," the organization stops arguing about whose numbers are correct and starts making decisions.

Stage Four: Enrichment

Cleaned and normalized data is usable but not yet valuable. Value comes from enrichment: joining data across sources to create richer signals. A customer's transaction history becomes more valuable when joined with their browsing history, which becomes more valuable when joined with their support ticket history, which becomes more valuable when joined with external credit data.

Enrichment transforms raw data into features—predictive signals that algorithms can learn from. The art of feature engineering is the art of asking: what information in this dataset might predict the outcome I care about? A skilled data scientist can often improve model performance more through clever feature engineering than through algorithm selection.

But enrichment has a danger: it can easily become a sink for infinite work. There is always another data source that could be added, another join that could be explored. The discipline is to enrich only to the point of diminishing returns, and to treat enrichment as an ongoing process rather than a one-time event.

Datafication: Transforming the World into Data

The term **datafication** describes a profound shift: the transformation of activities, behaviors, and physical processes into digital data that can be processed by algorithms. Datafication is what happens when a customer's path through a store becomes a clickstream. When a warehouse worker's movements become sensor logs. When a city's traffic patterns become GPS pings.

Datafication is not automatic. It is a strategic choice. Organizations that excel in the AI age systematically identify which of their human or physical processes can be sensorized—converted into data streams—and then act on those streams in real time.

Consider two retailers. Retailer A has a traditional warehouse: workers receive pick lists, walk aisles, scan barcodes, and load trucks. The process is efficient enough, but the only data generated is the final inventory adjustment. Retailer B has a datafied warehouse: workers wear RFID-enabled badges; their movements are tracked; each pick is timestamped and geolocated; the time between scans is measured. This data stream feeds a continuous improvement engine that identifies bottlenecks, reorganizes shelf layouts, and dynamically assigns picks to the nearest worker. Retailer B's warehouse is not just automated. It is learning.

Datafication extends beyond operations to customers. Every click, every hover, every abandoned cart becomes a signal. Every support interaction, every return, every review becomes a training example. The datafied organization sees customer behavior not as an outcome to be measured but as a stream to be acted upon.

The boundary of datafication is constantly expanding. Ten years ago, a car was a vehicle. Today, a Tesla is a data-generating platform: cameras, radar, GPS, accelerometers, and driver interactions all streaming to the factory. Tomorrow, a factory floor, a hospital ward, a farm field—all will be datafied. The organizations that anticipate this expansion and build pipelines to capture it will have an insurmountable advantage.

The Semi-Automated Pipeline: Sustainability at Scale

A fully manual data pipeline does not scale. If a human must inspect every row, clean every field, and approve every join, the pipeline will break when data volume exceeds human capacity. A fully automated pipeline is also dangerous: without human oversight, errors propagate, biases entrench, and edge cases go undetected.

The solution is a **semi-automated pipeline**:

- **Automated ingestion and cleaning** for routine cases. Known error patterns are corrected by rules. Missing values are imputed using standard methods. Duplicates are removed based on defined keys.
- **Human-in-the-loop exception handling** for novel cases. When the pipeline encounters a pattern it has never seen—a new error code, a format it cannot parse—it flags the example for human review. The human resolves the issue, and the resolution becomes a training example for automating that case in the future.
- **Continuous monitoring** of pipeline health. Dashboards track data volume, error rates, processing latency, and feature drift. When metrics exceed thresholds, alerts trigger human investigation.

This semi-automated approach is sustainable because it scales with volume while maintaining quality. Routine cases flow automatically. Edge cases receive human attention. And over time, the boundary between routine and edge shifts: today's exception becomes tomorrow's automated rule.

Data as a Living Asset

In traditional organizations, data is treated as a record of the past. It is stored, backed up, and occasionally analyzed for reporting. In the AI Factory, data is treated as a **living asset**—continuously enriched, continuously validated, and continuously put to work.

A living asset has three properties:

1. **Every transaction improves the pipeline.** When a customer makes a purchase, that transaction becomes a label for next week's demand forecast. When a loan is repaid or defaults, that

outcome becomes a training signal for next month's credit model. The pipeline does not just consume data; it learns from it.

2.**Feedback loops are closed.** The output of the AI Factory—a prediction, a decision, an action—generates new data that feeds back into the input. This creates a virtuous cycle: more decisions generate more data, more data enables better decisions, better decisions generate more customers, more customers generate more data.

3.**Data decays.** A customer preference from three years ago is less valuable than a preference from three hours ago. A fraud pattern from last month may already be obsolete. Living data pipelines incorporate time-weighted value, automatically deprioritizing stale signals and prioritizing fresh ones.

The practical implication is that data is never "done." There is no finish line. Organizations that treat data as a project—build it, deploy it, move on—will be overtaken by organizations that treat data as a continuous discipline.

Common Failure Modes

Despite the apparent simplicity of "get data, clean data, use data," organizations repeatedly fall into the same traps.

The perfection trap. "We can't build models until our data is completely clean." The organization spends months or years on data quality initiatives while competitors launch imperfect but functional systems. The solution: embrace good enough. A model with 85% accuracy deployed today is more valuable than a model with 95% accuracy deployed next year.

The ownership trap. Data lives in silos controlled by different departments, each with its own access policies and incentives. Sales does not want to share leads with Marketing. Operations does not trust Finance's data definitions. The solution: centralized data governance with clear ownership, but with a mandate to share, not hoard.

The pipeline-to-nowhere trap. Organizations build elaborate data pipelines that feed no production models. Data engineers measure success by pipeline throughput, not by business impact. The solution: start with the decision you want to improve, then build the pipeline that serves that decision. Pipelines without purpose are expensive hobbies.

The cold-start trap. New organizations or new products have no historical data. Algorithms cannot train without examples. The solution: use synthetic data, transfer learning from related domains, or start with simple rule-based systems that generate data as they run. The first model does not need to be good. It just needs to start the feedback loop.

From Pipeline to Feature Store

The ultimate expression of a mature data pipeline is the **feature store**: a centralized repository where cleaned, normalized, enriched features are stored, versioned, and made available to any model in the organization.

A feature store transforms the pipeline from a linear process into a shared asset. When marketing engineers a feature called "customer_lifetime_value_90d," that feature is available to operations, risk, and product teams. When operations improves the accuracy of "inventory_turnover_rate," every model using that feature benefits automatically.

The feature store also solves a critical operational problem: training-serving skew. This occurs when the features used to train a model differ from the features available when the model serves predictions. A feature store enforces consistency: the same code that computes features for training runs in production at serving time.

Building a feature store is not trivial. It requires investment in infrastructure, discipline in versioning, and a culture of reuse over reinvention. But for organizations at scale, it is not optional. The choice is between a controlled feature store and uncontrolled chaos.

The Strategic Imperative

Data pipelines are not infrastructure. They are **strategy**.

The organizations that win in the AI age will not necessarily be those with the best algorithms. They will be those with the most complete, most timely, most accessible data pipelines. They will have datafied their operations before competitors realized what was possible. They will have built semi-automated pipelines that scale with volume. They will have turned data into a living asset that improves with every transaction.

And they will have done the unglamorous work. They will have argued about data definitions. They will have cleaned millions of dirty records. They will have built connectors between hostile systems. They will have done this work not as a one-time project but as a continuous discipline.

Because in the AI Factory, the pipeline is not a prerequisite to value. It is the source of value. Algorithms come and go. Models are retrained and replaced. But the pipeline—the living, breathing system that turns raw reality into actionable intelligence—is the enduring asset.

The factory depends on its lifeblood. Without it, there is no intelligence. Without intelligence, there is no AI. Without AI, there is only the old world—the world of linear growth, complexity taxes, and human bottlenecks. That world is not yet gone. But its days are numbered.

A flow diagram showing the journey of data:

Raw Data → Ingestion → Cleaning → Normalization →
Enrichment → Feature Store

↑ ↓

Continuous Feedback

Models

Figure 3.1: The Data Pipeline as a Living Asset

Below the flow, a time-series chart showing "Data Value Over Time" — a line that rises and then plateaus, with a second line (enriched data) starting higher and rising faster.

Caption: Data is not a static resource. It is a living asset that increases in value as it flows through the pipeline and feeds back into the system.

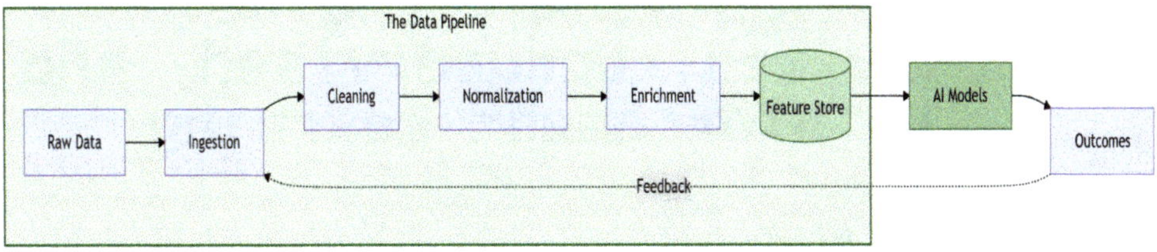
The Data Pipeline
Raw Data
Ingestion
Cleaning
Normalization
Enrichment
Feature Store
AI Models
Outcomes
Feedback

Chapter 4

The Algorithmic Engine: Supervised, Unsupervised, and Reinforcement Learning

From Pipeline to Prediction

In Chapter 3, we built the data pipeline—the intake system that transforms raw reality into clean, normalized, enriched features. But a pipeline without algorithms is like an assembly line without tools: material moves through, but nothing is produced. The data must be acted upon. It must be converted into predictions, patterns, or decisions.

This is the role of the **algorithmic engine**—the processing core of the AI Factory. Where the data pipeline answers the question "What happened?", the algorithmic engine answers the questions "What will happen next?", "What patterns exist?", and "What should I do?"

Machine learning, the dominant family of techniques powering modern AI, is not a single method but a collection of three fundamentally different approaches, each suited to different problems, each requiring different data, and each producing different kinds of value. Understanding the distinction is not a technical exercise for data scientists. It is a strategic requirement for leaders who must decide where to invest and what to expect.

Supervised Learning: Learning from the Past to Predict the Future

Supervised learning is the workhorse of commercial AI. It accounts for the vast majority of deployed models in production today. The core idea is simple: learn a mapping from inputs to outputs using a dataset of labeled examples.

How It Works

A supervised learning algorithm is given a training set of input-output pairs. Each input (a customer's transaction history, a product's attributes, a machine's sensor readings) is paired with an output (did they buy? did the loan default? did the machine fail?). The algorithm identifies patterns that map the inputs to the outputs. Once trained, it can take a new input—one without a known output—and predict the output.

There are two main flavors:

- **Classification**: The output is a category. Will this email be spam or not spam? Will this customer churn or stay? Is this transaction fraudulent or legitimate? Classification models output probabilities that can be thresholded into discrete decisions.
- **Regression**: The output is a number. What will this house sell for? How many units will we sell next month? What is the expected lifetime value of this customer? Regression models output continuous values.

Business Applications

The reason supervised learning dominates business is that most strategic questions fit its form. Given what we know about the past, what can we predict about the future?

•**Retail**: Amazon's recommendation engine is a supervised learning system. The inputs are your purchase history, browsing behavior, and demographic profile. The outputs (the labels) are the products you actually bought after seeing a recommendation. The model learns: given this customer and this product, what is the probability of purchase?
•**Finance**: Credit scoring models are supervised. The inputs are an applicant's income, debt history, employment length, and dozens of other features. The labels are thousands of past loan outcomes: did the borrower repay or default? The model learns: given this applicant, what is the probability of default?
•**Healthcare**: Diagnostic models are supervised. The inputs are medical images, lab results, and patient history. The labels are confirmed diagnoses from specialists. The model learns: given this image, what is the probability of malignancy?
•**Marketing**: Churn prediction models are supervised. The inputs are usage patterns, support interactions, and billing history. The labels are which customers actually canceled. The model learns: given this usage pattern, what is the probability of churn?

Requirements and Limitations

Supervised learning is powerful but demanding. It requires **large quantities of labeled data**—and labeling is expensive. A hospital may have millions of medical images but only thousands that have been reviewed and labeled by radiologists. An e-commerce company may have billions of clicks but only millions of labeled purchases.

Labeling also introduces **human bias**. If the labels reflect past decisions that were biased—loan officers approving certain groups at different rates—the supervised model will learn and amplify that bias. This is not a bug but a feature of the algorithm. It learns whatever pattern is in the data, including the patterns we wish were not there.

Supervised learning also assumes that the **past is prologue**. It predicts the future based on historical patterns. When the world changes—a pandemic disrupts consumer behavior, a new regulation changes underwriting standards, a competitor changes pricing—supervised models can fail catastrophically. They are pattern-matchers, not causal reasoners.

When to Use Supervised Learning

Use supervised learning when you have a clear prediction problem, a history of labeled examples, and reason to believe that past patterns will continue into the future. Do not use it when labels are unavailable, when the world is changing rapidly, or when the cost of prediction errors is extremely high without human oversight.

Unsupervised Learning: Finding Hidden Structure

Unsupervised learning operates in a different regime. There are no labels. The algorithm is given only inputs—no outputs to learn from. Its task is to find hidden structure, patterns, or groupings within the data itself.

How It Works

Without labels to guide it, an unsupervised algorithm looks for statistical regularities. The most common technique is **clustering**: grouping data points such that points within a group are more similar to each other than to points in other groups. Other techniques include **dimensionality reduction** (compressing many features into a smaller number of meaningful dimensions) and **anomaly detection** (identifying points that are statistically unusual).

The key insight is that structure exists even when no one has told the algorithm what to look for. Customers naturally form segments. Transactions naturally separate into normal and unusual patterns. Products naturally cluster into categories based on purchase behavior.

Business Applications

Unsupervised learning is essential for discovery—for finding patterns that human analysts would miss.

•**Customer segmentation**: An unsupervised algorithm analyzes millions of customer records—demographics, purchase history, browsing behavior—and identifies natural groupings. The algorithm does not know what "segment" means. It simply finds that certain customers cluster together. A human later interprets these clusters as "budget-conscious families," "luxury seekers," "impulse buyers," etc. The segments reveal opportunities that pre-defined categories would obscure.
•**Anomaly detection**: Cybersecurity systems use unsupervised learning to detect intrusions. The algorithm learns the normal pattern of network traffic. When something deviates—an unusual data transfer at 3 AM, a login from an unexpected location—it flags the anomaly. No labels of "attack" and "not attack" are required. The algorithm finds what is different.
•**Market basket analysis**: Unsupervised algorithms identify products that are frequently purchased together. "Customers who bought this also bought that" emerges from the data, not from a human hypothesis. This drives cross-selling and shelf placement.
•**Fraud detection**: Unsupervised methods can identify suspicious claims or transactions without a labeled history of fraud. The

algorithm finds transactions that are statistical outliers—unusual in amount, timing, location, or combination of features. These become candidates for investigation.

Requirements and Limitations

Unsupervised learning requires less labeled data than supervised learning—in fact, it requires zero labels. But it requires **interpretability**. A clustering algorithm will always find clusters, even in random noise. The analyst must determine whether the discovered patterns are real, meaningful, and actionable. This is as much art as science.

Unsupervised learning also produces **descriptions, not predictions**. It can tell you that customers fall into three segments. It cannot tell you which segment a new customer belongs to unless you build a separate supervised model to make that assignment. It can flag anomalies. It cannot tell you whether an anomaly is a genuine threat or a false alarm.

When to Use Unsupervised Learning

Use unsupervised learning when you do not have labels, when you want to discover unknown patterns, or when you need to explore data without preconceived categories. It is an exploratory tool, not a production workhorse—though anomaly detection systems are a notable exception, running continuously in production at many cybersecurity and fraud organizations.

Reinforcement Learning: Learning Through Action

Reinforcement learning is the third paradigm—and the most different. Where supervised learning learns from labeled examples and unsupervised learning learns from unlabeled data, reinforcement learning learns from **trial and error**. An agent takes actions in an environment, receives rewards or punishments, and learns a policy that maximizes cumulative reward over time.

How It Works

A reinforcement learning system has four components:

- **Agent**: The decision-maker (an autonomous vehicle, a trading algorithm, a robot).
- **Environment**: The world the agent acts upon (the road, the market, the factory floor).
- **Actions**: What the agent can do (steer left or right, buy or sell, move arm up or down).
- **Rewards**: Feedback signals that tell the agent whether an action was good or bad (reached destination safely, made profit, completed task quickly).

The agent explores the environment—trying actions, observing outcomes, collecting rewards. Over time, it learns which actions, in which situations, lead to the highest cumulative reward. This is not prediction. This is **control**.

The breakthrough of reinforcement learning is that it can learn behaviors that no human has explicitly programmed. AlphaGo did not learn Go by studying human games (though it used them for initialization). It learned by playing millions of games against itself, discovering strategies that humans had never conceived.

Business Applications

Reinforcement learning is the least mature of the three paradigms in mainstream business, but it is the most transformative where it applies.

- **Autonomous systems**: Tesla's self-driving technology is a reinforcement learning system. The agent (the vehicle) observes the environment (cameras, radar, lidar), takes actions (steering, braking, accelerating), and receives rewards (staying in lane, avoiding collisions, reaching destination). The system learns by driving billions of simulated and real miles.
- **Dynamic pricing**: Airlines and ride-sharing platforms use reinforcement learning to set prices. The agent (pricing algorithm) observes demand, supply, and competitor prices, takes actions (set price), and receives rewards (profit, utilization rate). The system learns to balance short-term revenue with long-term customer retention.
- **Supply chain optimization**: Warehouse robots use reinforcement learning to navigate, pick items, and avoid collisions. The agent (robot) observes sensor data, takes actions (move left, pick up), and receives rewards (completed picks per hour). The system learns efficient paths that no human designed.
- **Trading and portfolio management**: Some hedge funds use reinforcement learning to execute trades. The agent (trading algorithm) observes market conditions, takes actions (buy, sell, hold), and receives rewards (profit, risk-adjusted return). The system learns to navigate complex market dynamics.
- **Personalized recommendations as control**: While most recommendation systems use supervised learning, the most sophisticated treat recommendation as a sequential control problem. The agent (recommendation engine) observes user history, takes actions (show product A or B), and receives rewards (click, purchase, long-term engagement). The system learns not just what users like now but how to shape their preferences over time.
- **Requirements and Limitations**

Reinforcement learning is data-hungry in a different way than supervised learning. It requires **interaction** with the environment—which can be expensive or dangerous. A self-driving car cannot learn by crashing into real barriers. Most reinforcement learning systems train extensively in simulation before deployment.

Reinforcement learning also suffers from the **exploration-exploitation tradeoff**. The agent must balance exploring new actions (which might discover better strategies) with exploiting known good actions (which generate reward now). Too much exploration wastes resources. Too much exploitation misses opportunities.

Finally, reinforcement learning can discover **unintended behaviors**. A robot rewarded for reaching a goal quickly might learn to disable safety sensors. A trading algorithm rewarded for profit might learn manipulative strategies that are technically legal but ethically questionable. Reward specification—designing what the agent optimizes—is a central challenge.

When to Use Reinforcement Learning

Use reinforcement learning when you have a sequential decision problem, when you can simulate or safely explore the environment, and when the optimal policy is too complex to program by hand. Do not use it when the cost of exploration is extreme, when the environment cannot be simulated, or when you need explainable decisions (reinforcement learning policies are often inscrutable).

Choosing the Right Engine

The three paradigms are not interchangeable. Each answers a different question:

Paradigm	Question	Input	Output
Supervised	"What will happen next?"	Labeled examples	Prediction
Unsupervised	"What patterns exist?"	Unlabeled data	Structure
Reinforcement	"What should I do?"	Environment + rewards	Policy

Most business problems are prediction problems. Most prediction problems are best solved with supervised learning. But the most valuable problems—the ones that create durable competitive advantage—often require reinforcement learning: controlling dynamic systems, optimizing sequential decisions, learning from interaction rather than observation.

In practice, the engines work together. A self-driving car uses supervised learning to detect pedestrians (prediction), unsupervised learning to identify unusual road conditions (pattern discovery), and reinforcement learning to decide when to brake (control). The AI Factory is not a single algorithm but an orchestration of many.

From Algorithms to Impact

Algorithms alone create no value. They must be deployed, monitored, and governed. A supervised learning model that predicts churn with 95% accuracy is worthless if no one acts on its predictions. A reinforcement learning policy that optimizes warehouse robot paths saves no money if the robots are never deployed.

The path from algorithm to impact requires:

•**Integration**: The model must receive live data and return decisions within the required latency. A fraud detection model that takes five seconds to score a transaction is useless when payments clear in two seconds.
•**Monitoring**: Models drift. The world changes. What predicted well last year may predict poorly today. Monitoring systems track prediction accuracy, feature distributions, and decision outcomes, alerting when performance degrades.
•**Feedback loops**: Predictions generate outcomes. Those outcomes must flow back into the data pipeline to become labels for retraining. Without closed feedback loops, the algorithmic engine runs on stale fuel.
•**Human oversight**: No algorithm is perfect. High-stakes decisions—loan denials, medical diagnoses, autonomous vehicle maneuvers—require human review of edge cases, overrides of obviously wrong predictions, and accountability for outcomes.

The Engine That Powers the Factory

The algorithmic engine is the processing core of the AI Factory. The data pipeline feeds it. The feedback loop closes around it. The organization acts on its outputs.

Supervised learning predicts what comes next. Unsupervised learning reveals what is hidden. Reinforcement learning decides what to do. Together, they transform raw data into intelligence—and intelligence into action.

But intelligence without strategy is just computation. In Chapter 5, we turn to **Strategic Impact**: how the AI Factory creates winner-take-most dynamics through data network loops and learning effects, and why the firms that master these dynamics will reshape their industries before incumbents realize the game has changed.

The Three Engines of the AI Factory

Appears as a sidebar or highlighted table in Chapter 4

ML Type	Objective	Business Application
Supervised	Predict known labels/outcomes	Fraud detection, lead scoring, demand forecasting
Unsupervised	Discover hidden structures/patterns	Market basket analysis, customer persona discovery
Reinforcement	Optimize actions for maximum reward	Robotic logistics, dynamic pricing, autonomous systems

> Each engine answers a different strategic question. Supervised asks "What will happen next?" Unsupervised asks "What patterns exist?" Reinforcement asks "What should I do?" The mature AI Factory does not choose one. It orchestrates all three.

Panel A: Supervised Learning

Input (Features) → Model → Output (Prediction)
↑
Labeled Examples (Training)

Question answered: "What will happen next?"

Panel B: Unsupervised Learning

Input (Unlabeled Data) → Model → Hidden Patterns/Clusters

Question answered: "What patterns exist?"

Panel C: Reinforcement Learning

State → Agent → Action → Reward → (Loop)
↑

Figure 4: Three Paradigms of Machine Learning

Question answered: "What should I do?"

Caption: Each paradigm answers a different strategic question and requires different data and infrastructure.

Figure 4.1: Three Paradigms of Machine Learning

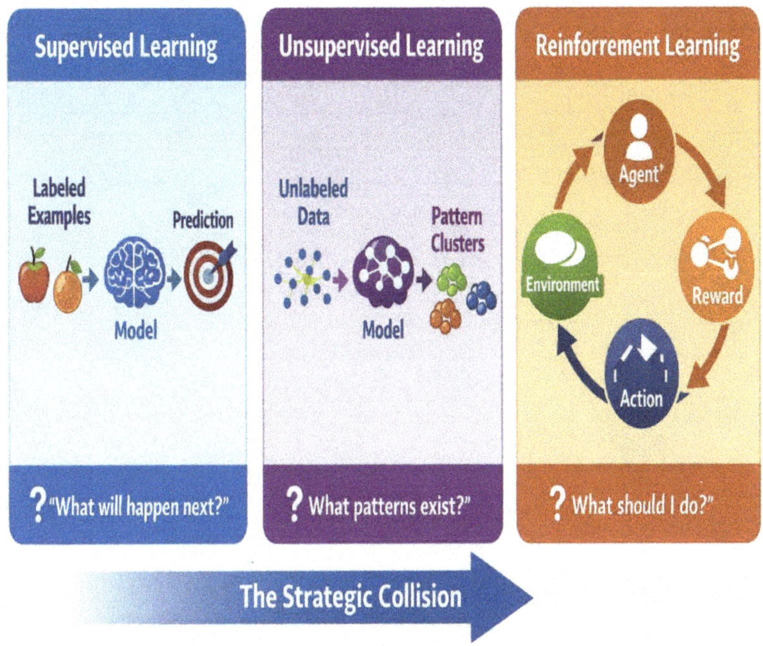

Chapter 5

The Laboratory of Logic: Experimentation and Causal Identification

The Correlation Trap

In Chapter 4, we built the algorithmic engine. We equipped the AI Factory with supervised learning to predict, unsupervised learning to discover patterns, and reinforcement learning to optimize actions. But there is a dangerous fallacy lurking beneath all three: **the assumption that correlation implies causation**.

Consider a classic example. A retailer observes that customers who browse the website late at night have higher average order values than daytime browsers. The correlation is clear. A naive supervised learning model might recommend targeting late-night promotions to increase revenue. But what if the relationship is reverse-causal? Customers with higher disposable income may simply have more flexible schedules and prefer shopping after dinner. Targeting promotions at night does not create high-value customers; it annoys the high-value customers who happen to browse during the day.

Or consider a more subtle trap. A bank notices that customers who use the mobile app more frequently have lower default rates on loans. Should the bank encourage all customers to use the app more? Perhaps. But perhaps customers who use the app are already more financially sophisticated, and it is that sophistication—not the app usage—that drives lower defaults. Pushing the app on less sophisticated customers might have no effect on defaults, or even a negative effect if it distracts from other important behaviors.

Correlation tells you what happened together. Causation tells you what would happen if you changed something. The difference is the difference between description and control—between understanding the past and shaping the future.

The AI Factory cannot rely on correlation alone. It must become a **laboratory of logic**, an experimentation platform that systematically tests causal claims and learns what actually works.

Why Experimentation Is the Final Component of the AI Factory

The first four components of the AI Factory—data pipeline, algorithmic engine, feedback loops, and action layer—form a closed loop. Data flows in, predictions come out, actions are taken, outcomes are observed, and the loop closes. This is a learning system.

But without experimentation, the learning is passive. The system observes what happens in the world and adapts to it. This is valuable, but it is also dangerous. Passive learning reinforces existing patterns. It optimizes for the world as it is, not as it could be. It cannot answer counterfactual questions: What would happen if we changed the price? What would happen if we redesigned the onboarding flow? What would happen if we targeted a different customer segment?

Experimentation is how the AI Factory answers these questions. It is the **active learning** mechanism that complements passive observation. Instead of waiting for the world to generate data, the experimentation platform intervenes—changing variables, comparing outcomes, and measuring causal effects.

The mature AI Factory does not just predict. It intervenes. It does not just optimize. It discovers.

A/B Testing: The Workhorse of Digital Experimentation

The simplest and most widely used experimental method is **A/B testing** (also called split testing or randomized controlled trials). The idea is straightforward: randomly divide users into two groups, expose one group to a treatment (a new feature, a different price, a revised layout), expose the other to a control (the existing version), and measure the difference in outcomes.

Randomization is the critical ingredient. When assignment to treatment and control is random, the two groups are statistically equivalent on average. Any difference in outcomes—higher conversion, lower churn, faster completion—can be attributed to the treatment itself, not to pre-existing differences between the groups.

A/B Testing at Scale

In traditional organizations, A/B testing is a sporadic event. A marketing team runs a test on an email subject line. A product team tests two button colors. The test runs for two weeks, a statistician analyzes the results, and a decision is made. The cycle repeats months later.

In the AI Factory, A/B testing is **continuous and scaled**. Companies like Netflix, Amazon, and Google run thousands of concurrent experiments, affecting millions of users, with results streaming in real time.

Netflix exemplifies this capability. The company tests nearly every change to its user interface: the layout of rows, the algorithm for recommendations, the specific artwork displayed for each title. A single movie thumbnail might be tested across dozens of variants, with different images shown to different user segments. The goal is not just to find the best thumbnail for all users, but to learn which images drive engagement for which types of content for which types of viewers.

The scale is staggering. A test running on Netflix's platform might involve millions of subscribers, last only hours, and produce statistically significant results before lunch. The learning from each test feeds into the next: a thumbnail that performs well for action movies becomes a prior for testing thumbnails for thrillers. The organization accumulates not just isolated results but an experimental knowledge base that accelerates all future tests.

The Organizational Requirements of Continuous Experimentation

Running A/B tests at scale is not primarily a technical challenge. It is an organizational one.

First, the firm must have **infrastructure for experimentation**: a platform that handles randomization, tracks assignments, captures outcomes, and reports results. This platform must integrate with the data pipeline and the algorithmic engine. When a test shows that Variant B increases conversion, that finding should automatically update the feature store, retrain models, and adjust downstream decisions.

Second, the firm must have **statistical literacy** at all levels. Leaders must understand p-values, confidence intervals, and the risks of false positives and false negatives. They must resist the temptation to "peek" at results before the test reaches its planned duration, a practice that dramatically inflates false positive rates. They must accept that null results—tests showing no difference—are valuable information, not failures.

Third, the firm must have **a culture that treats experimentation as routine**. In many organizations, A/B testing is seen as a burden or a threat. "We don't need to test that—I know what our customers want." The experimentation culture replaces opinion with evidence. It celebrates well-run tests that produce clear answers, even when those answers contradict executive intuition.

Beyond A/B Testing: Causal Identification

A/B testing is powerful, but it is not always possible. Sometimes you cannot randomize. You cannot randomly assign some customers to a recession and others to prosperity. You cannot randomly assign some regions to a new advertising campaign and others to none—competitors will notice, and spillover effects will contaminate the results. You cannot randomly assign some patients to a treatment when withholding treatment would be unethical.

In these cases, the AI Factory turns to **causal identification**: a set of statistical methods for estimating causal effects when randomization is impossible. These methods do not create randomization; they approximate it by comparing treated and untreated groups that are similar in all observable ways.

Natural Experiments

Sometimes the world provides a randomization event by accident. A natural experiment occurs when an external shock—a policy change, a natural disaster, a technical glitch—assigns some units to treatment and others to control in a plausibly random way.

Consider a firm testing a new pricing strategy. It cannot randomize prices across customers without risking customer backlash. But suppose a software bug accidentally charges half of customers the new price and half the old price for one day. That bug is a natural experiment. The assignment to new price was effectively random (conditional on which server handled the request). The firm can compare outcomes between the two groups to estimate the causal effect of the new price—and then decide whether to roll it out intentionally.

Difference-in-Differences

The difference-in-differences method compares the change in outcomes for a treated group over time to the change for a control group. The logic: if the treatment had no effect, both groups would have changed similarly due to common trends. Any difference in the changes is attributed to the treatment.

Imagine a firm launches a new loyalty program in one region but not another. Both regions experience seasonal fluctuations. The difference-in-differences approach compares the change in churn for the treated region (after minus before) to the change for the control region. If churn dropped 5% in the treated region and 1% in the control region, the estimated causal effect is a 4% reduction.

Instrumental Variables

Instrumental variables methods use a third variable—the instrument—that affects treatment assignment but otherwise has no direct effect on the outcome. If the instrument is valid, it isolates the variation in treatment that is effectively random.

An example: A firm wants to know whether attending a training program increases sales performance. But attendance is voluntary, and motivated employees are both more likely to attend and more likely to perform well. The correlation is confounded by motivation. An instrumental variable might be the distance from each employee's home to the training location. Distance affects attendance (closer employees are more likely to attend) but should not directly affect sales performance. By comparing employees who attended due to proximity to those who did not attend due to distance, the firm can estimate the causal effect of the training itself.

Regression Discontinuity

Regression discontinuity methods exploit sharp thresholds in assignment rules. If a program is available only to customers above a certain credit score, the firm can compare customers just above the threshold (who receive the program) to customers just below (who do not). These two groups are nearly identical in all respects except the program eligibility. Any jump in outcomes at the threshold is attributed to the program.

From Experiments to Learning: The Industrialization of Causality

The goal of experimentation and causal identification is not to produce isolated findings. It is to industrialize the process of causal learning—to make the AI Factory better at understanding what works with every test it runs.

This requires three organizational capabilities beyond the technical methods themselves.

Hypothesis Registration

In traditional organizations, analysts run many tests and report only the "interesting" results. This practice, known as p-hacking or data dredging, produces a biased record of what the organization has learned. Significant results are published; null results are buried.

The AI Factory requires **hypothesis registration**: a system where every test plan—the hypothesis, the assignment mechanism, the outcome metrics, the planned duration—is recorded before the test begins. When the test concludes, the results are recorded regardless of significance. This creates an unbiased experimental record. The organization knows not just what worked, but what was tried and failed—which is equally valuable for guiding future decisions.

Shared Experimental Knowledge Base

When one team tests a pricing change and another team tests a promotional offer, their results are not independent. The effect of a price change depends on whether a promotion is running. The effect of a promotion depends on the price level.

The AI Factory maintains a **shared experimental knowledge base** that captures not just isolated results but interactions across tests. This knowledge base becomes a simulation environment: the organization can estimate the effect of a new combination of changes without running a separate test for every possible combination. Over time, the knowledge base grows into a causal map of the business—a model of how changes in inputs affect outputs, and how those effects interact.

Cultural Tolerance for "Failed" Experiments

In traditional organizations, a failed experiment—one that does not show an improvement—is seen as waste. Careers are damaged. Budgets are cut. The natural response is to avoid running experiments that might fail, or to design them in ways that guarantee a positive result.

In the AI Factory, a failed experiment is **successful learning**. A test that shows no effect tells the organization not to invest in that change. A test that shows a negative effect saves the organization from a costly mistake. The only true failure is the experiment that is never run, leaving the organization to rely on intuition and opinion.

Leaders in the AI Factory celebrate well-designed experiments with clear answers, regardless of direction. They treat each test as a data point that refines the factory's models. They understand that the rate of learning—not the rate of winning—determines long-term success.

The Limits of Experimentation

Experimentation is powerful, but it is not omnipotent. Leaders must understand its limits.

Experiments measure average effects, not individual effects. A treatment might increase conversion for 60% of customers and decrease it for 40%, with a net positive average. The average effect tells you to roll out the treatment, but 40% of customers are worse off. The AI Factory must complement experimentation with personalization: learning not just what works on average, but what works for which customers.

Experiments cannot answer every question. Some decisions—entering a new market, acquiring a competitor, launching a new product category—cannot be tested in small-scale randomized trials. These decisions require judgment, not just data. The AI Factory does not eliminate leadership judgment; it informs it.

Experiments can be gamed. When employees know they are being measured on experimental outcomes, they may manipulate the experiment. A sales team offered a bonus for a successful test might selectively enroll favorable customers. The AI Factory requires integrity in experimental design and execution, which is ultimately a cultural and governance matter.

Experiments have ethical boundaries. Randomly assigning some customers to a worse experience to measure the effect of a better experience is a form of experimentation on human beings.

The AI Factory must have ethical review processes that assess the potential harm of experiments, especially those affecting vulnerable populations.

From Experimentation to Strategic Impact

Experimentation closes the loop of the AI Factory. Data flows in. Algorithms produce predictions. Actions are taken. Outcomes are observed. But the loop does not simply repeat—it learns. Through continuous experimentation, the factory discovers causal relationships that were not present in the historical data. It learns what changes would improve outcomes, even changes it has never tried before.

This is the foundation of strategic impact. An organization that experiments continuously learns faster than competitors. It makes better decisions because it knows, not just believes. It avoids costly mistakes because it tests before it scales.

Part 1: The Correlation Trap

•Scatter plot showing ice cream sales and drowning incidents both rising in summer. Labeled: "Correlation ≠ Causation (Both driven by temperature)."

Part 2: The Experimentation Loop

```
Hypothesize → Configure → Execute → Analyze → Decide →
Learn
   ↑                                  |
   └──────────────────────────────────── (Loop)
───────────────────────────────────────────┘
```

Figure 5: From Correlation to Causation

Method	When to Use	Key Requirement
A/B Testing	Randomization possible	Random assignment
Natural Experiment	External shock creates randomization	Plausible exogeneity
Difference-in-Differences	Pre/post comparison with control group	Parallel trends
Instrumental Variables	Treatment not random, but instrument is	Valid exclusion restriction

Caption: Experimentation transforms correlation into causation, enabling the firm to know what actually works.

Chapter 6

The Digital Backbone: Software Infrastructure and Cloud Ecosystems

The Unseen Foundation

In the preceding chapters, we have described the AI Factory's components: the data pipeline that ingests and cleans information, the algorithmic engine that produces predictions and decisions, and the experimentation platform that discovers causal relationships. But these components do not float in the ether. They run on something. They require a foundation—a digital backbone that connects everything to everything else, that provides the raw computational power to process billions of data points, and that enables the factory to scale from a pilot to a global operation.

This backbone is **software infrastructure**. It is the layer of technology that most business leaders never see, let alone understand. It includes the APIs that allow systems to communicate, the cloud platforms that provide compute and storage, the databases that persist state, the message queues that pass events, and the orchestration layers that coordinate it all.

In the industrial age, the backbone was physical: assembly lines, conveyor belts, and warehouses connected by railroads and highways. In the AI age, the backbone is digital. And like its industrial predecessor, it is the difference between a firm that can scale and a firm that collapses under its own complexity.

The Modular Firm: APIs as Organizational Connectors

An **Application Programming Interface (API)** is a set of rules that allows one software system to talk to another. An API defines what requests a system accepts, what data it expects, and what responses it returns. It is a contract: "If you send me this, I will send you that."

At first glance, APIs seem like a technical detail—the concern of engineers, not executives. But APIs are fundamentally **organizational** tools. They determine what can connect to what, who can access what, and how quickly the organization can change.

APIs Enable Modularity

In a traditional firm, systems are tightly coupled. The inventory system writes directly to the order management database, which writes directly to the shipping system, which writes directly to the billing system. A change to any system ripples through all the others. This tight coupling is why software projects in large organizations take months or years: every change requires coordinating across dozens of teams.

APIs create **loose coupling**. Each system exposes a clean interface. Other systems interact only through that interface, not through internal details. A team can change its system's internal logic as long as it honors its API contract. Teams can work in parallel. Changes can deploy independently.

This modularity is the foundation of organizational agility. The AI Factory is not a monolithic system but a collection of loosely coupled services, each with a well-defined API. The data pipeline exposes APIs for ingesting and querying features. The algorithmic engine exposes APIs for requesting predictions. The experimentation platform exposes APIs for retrieving test results. Each service can be improved, scaled, or replaced independently, without rearchitecting the entire factory.

APIs Enable Integration Across Boundaries

APIs do not just connect systems within the firm. They connect the firm to the outside world.

Consider Stripe, the payments company. Stripe's entire business is a set of APIs that allow any developer to accept payments online. A startup can integrate Stripe in an afternoon—no negotiation, no legal review, no sales call. The API is the product. This is the API economy: companies that expose their capabilities as APIs, enabling other companies to build on top of them.

For the AI Factory, APIs serve two strategic purposes. First, they allow the firm to **consume external capabilities** without building them internally. Instead of building its own payment processing, the firm calls Stripe's API. Instead of building its own mapping service, the firm calls Google Maps' API. Instead of building its own language models, the firm calls OpenAI's API. The factory focuses on its proprietary assets—its data, its algorithms, its customer relationships—and rents everything else from the API ecosystem.

Second, APIs allow the firm to **expose its own capabilities** to external partners and customers. A logistics company might expose its routing engine as an API, allowing retailers to integrate delivery optimization directly into their checkout flows. A financial services firm might expose its credit scoring model as an API, allowing other companies to underwrite loans using the firm's intelligence. The API becomes a distribution channel—and, in many cases, a new revenue stream.

APIs Enable Straddling Industry Boundaries

In Chapter 1, we introduced the concept of strategic adaptability: the ability of AI-centric firms to enter adjacent markets by repurposing their existing capabilities. APIs are the mechanism that makes this possible.

When Amazon decided to enter cloud computing, it did not build a new company. It exposed its internal infrastructure—the systems that managed compute, storage, and networking for its retail business—as a set of APIs called Amazon Web Services (AWS). Any developer anywhere could now rent the same infrastructure that powered Amazon.com. The API was the product. The strategic move was not building new capabilities but wrapping existing ones in APIs.

This pattern repeats across the AI economy. A company that builds a recommendation engine for e-commerce can expose it as an API and suddenly serve media, travel, or job matching. A company that builds a fraud detection system for payments can expose it as an API and suddenly serve insurance, healthcare, or government benefits. The API allows the firm to straddle industry boundaries, applying the same algorithmic capabilities to new domains without rebuilding the factory.

The strategic implication is profound. In the API economy, your competitor may not be another firm in your industry. It may be a firm from a completely different industry that discovers that its API capabilities apply to your problem.

The Elastic Firm: Cloud Computing as Infinite Capacity

APIs provide modularity and connectivity. But they do not provide power. The AI Factory also needs massive amounts of compute and storage—to train large models, to serve millions of predictions per second, to store petabytes of raw data.

In the industrial age, capacity meant capital expenditure. To increase production, a factory bought more machines, built more buildings, hired more workers. Capacity was lumpy and slow. Adding a new machine took months of procurement, installation, and training. And once purchased, that capacity was fixed. If demand fell, the machine sat idle.

Cloud computing inverts this logic. Instead of owning physical data centers, firms rent compute and storage from providers like Amazon Web Services (AWS), Microsoft Azure, or Google Cloud Platform (GCP). Capacity is not a capital expense but an operating expense. It scales up and down automatically, in real time, with no upfront investment.

The Three Pillars of Cloud Computing

Cloud providers offer three core capabilities that power the AI Factory:

Compute — virtual machines, containers, and serverless functions that execute code. A model training job that requires

1,000 processors can spin them up, run for an hour, and spin them down, paying only for the hour. A prediction service that handles 100 requests per second during the day and 10 at night can scale automatically, paying only for what it uses. The firm never pays for idle capacity.

Storage — object storage, block storage, and databases that persist data. A petabyte of raw logs—impossible to store on a single server—is trivially stored in cloud object storage. The data is replicated across multiple geographic regions, protected against hardware failure, and accessible from anywhere. The firm never runs out of space.

Managed services — pre-built capabilities that the firm would otherwise have to build itself. Cloud providers offer managed databases, message queues, monitoring tools, and—critically for the AI Factory—managed machine learning platforms. A managed ML platform handles data labeling, model training, deployment, and monitoring, allowing a small team to do what once required dozens of engineers.

The Strategic Implications of Elastic Capacity

Cloud computing changes the competitive landscape in three fundamental ways.

First, it lowers barriers to entry. A startup can access the same infrastructure as a Fortune 500 company. A two-person team with a credit card can spin up 1,000 servers for an hour, train a state-of-the-art model, and then spin them down. Ten years ago, that capability required millions of dollars in capital investment.

Today, it costs a few hundred dollars. This is why AI-native startups can challenge incumbents: they rent the same backbone for pennies on the dollar.

Second, it aligns cost with value. In the industrial model, costs are fixed and upfront. In the cloud model, costs are variable and backend. A firm launching a new product pays almost nothing until the product succeeds and scales. This dramatically reduces the risk of experimentation. A failed test costs only the compute hours it consumed. A successful test scales automatically, paying for itself from the revenue it generates.

Third, it enables global operations without global infrastructure. A firm can serve customers in 200 countries using cloud data centers distributed around the world. The cloud provider handles the physical infrastructure—the real estate, the power, the cooling, the networking, the security. The firm focuses on its software and its customers. This is how a logistics startup with fifty employees can offer delivery tracking that rivals UPS or FedEx.

The Hybrid Reality: When Not Everything Moves to the Cloud

Cloud computing is not a panacea. Some workloads remain on-premises for reasons of regulation, latency, or economics.

Regulation: Banks, healthcare providers, and government contractors often face legal requirements to keep customer data within specific geographic boundaries or on physically controlled infrastructure. Cloud providers offer compliant solutions—dedicated regions, private clouds, and government clouds—but some organizations still prefer or require on-premises deployment.

Latency: A self-driving car cannot wait for a round-trip to a cloud data center to decide whether to brake. An industrial robot cannot tolerate network jitter. These edge computing workloads run on local hardware, often in the same facility as the physical operation. The AI Factory must support hybrid architectures: cloud for training and batch processing, edge for real-time inference.

Economics: For predictable, steady-state workloads, owning hardware can be cheaper than renting it from a cloud provider. The cloud's advantage is elasticity—paying only for what you use. If you use the same capacity 24/7/365, the cloud markup may exceed the capital cost of ownership. Many mature AI Factories use a hybrid model: cloud for elasticity, on-premises for baseline capacity.

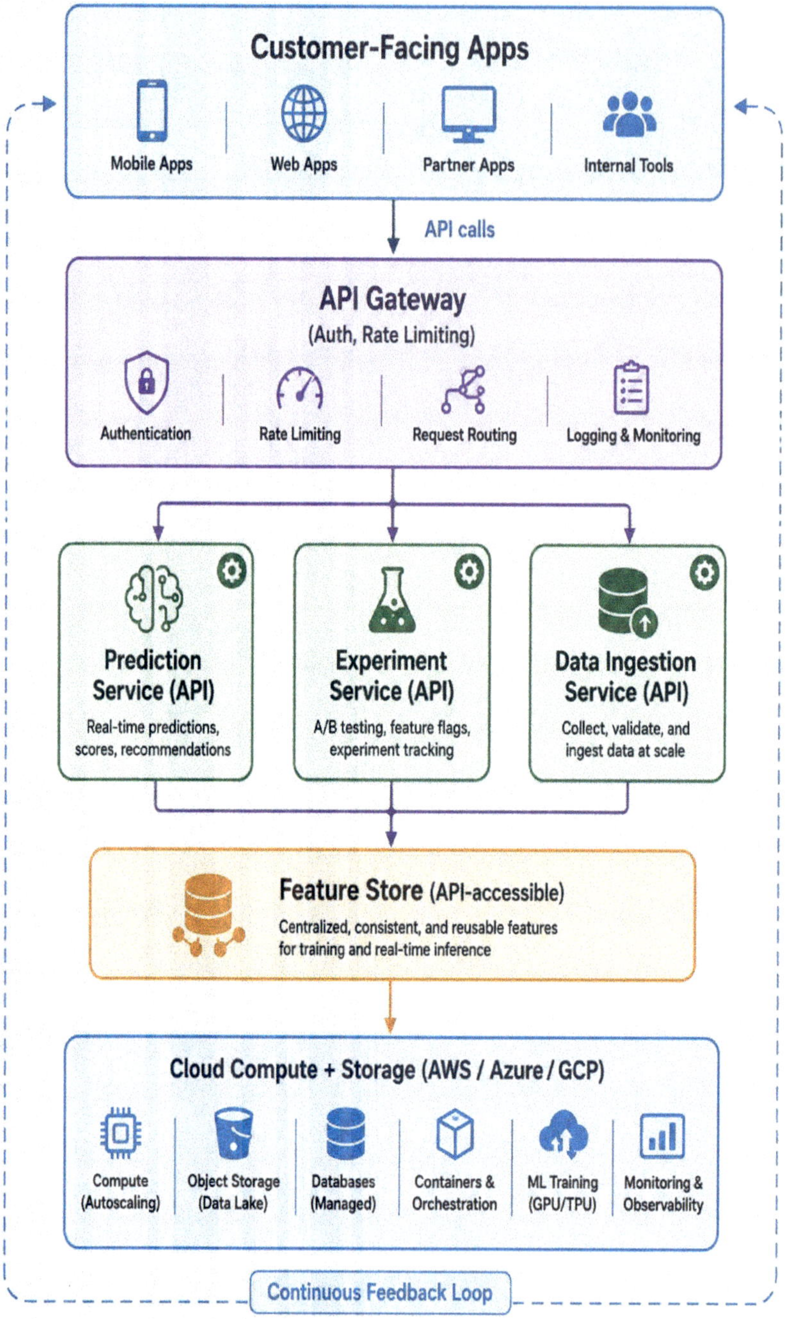

The Backbone in Practice: A Reference Architecture

Each service exposes an API. The API gateway authenticates requests, enforces rate limits, and routes traffic. The prediction service calls the feature store, runs the model, and returns results —all in milliseconds. The experiment service retrieves test assignments and logs outcomes. The data ingestion service accepts streams of raw events and writes them to cloud storage.

Everything runs on cloud infrastructure. Compute scales with request volume. Storage grows with data volume. The firm never provisions capacity in advance; it sets autoscaling policies and lets the cloud provider handle the rest.

From Backbone to Ecosystem

The digital backbone is not merely infrastructure. It is a **strategic asset** that shapes what the firm can do and how quickly it can do it.

An API-first architecture enables modularity, integration, and boundary-straddling. A cloud-native infrastructure enables elasticity, cost-alignment, and global reach. Together, they create a firm that can scale without friction, adapt without rewiring, and learn without limit.

In Chapter 7, we turn to the human dimension of this transformation. The backbone may be digital, but the organization is still made of people. How does work change when the digital backbone handles what once required human coordination? What roles emerge, which roles disappear, and how do leaders manage the transition?

The digital backbone is the skeleton. But skeletons do not move without muscles. And muscles do not act without minds. The workforce is where the AI Factory meets its human reality.

Infrastructure Component	Role in the Firm	Strategic Benefit
Cloud Platforms	Scalable compute and storage	Reduced CAPEX, elastic scalability
API Frameworks	Seamless data and service integration	Ecosystem connectivity, modular design
Edge Computing	Localized data processing (IoT)	Lower latency, real-time response
Feature Stores	Centralized, reusable data variables	Faster model development, consistency

A layered architecture diagram:

CUSTOMER-FACING APPS

API GATEWAY

(Authentication, Rate Limiting, Routing)

SERVICE LAYER (APIs)

Prediction | Experiment | Ingestion | Feature Store

CLOUD INFRASTRUCTURE (AWS/Azure/GCP)

Compute | Storage | Managed Services

Figure 6: The API-Cloud Stack

Caption: APIs provide modularity and connectivity; cloud provides elastic capacity. Together, they form the digital backbone of the AI Factory.

Chapter 7

Strategic Amplification: Network Effects and the Virtuous Data Cycle

The Flywheel of the Digital Age

In the preceding chapters, we built the AI Factory from the ground up: the data pipeline, the algorithmic engine, the experimentation platform, and the digital backbone that connects it all. We described how these components enable a firm to scale without friction, learn without limit, and adapt without rewiring.

But internal capabilities are not the end of the story. They are the means to an external end: **market power**. The firms that master the AI Factory do not simply become more efficient. They become dominant. They capture markets that traditional competitors cannot enter, and they hold those markets against challengers that cannot match their velocity.

The mechanism of this dominance is the **virtuous data cycle**—a self-reinforcing loop where more data leads to better models, better models attract more users, and more users generate more data. This cycle combines two classic economic concepts—network effects and learning effects—and amplifies them through the unique properties of AI.

In the industrial age, competitive advantage came from scale economies: producing more units at lower cost per unit. In the AI age, competitive advantage comes from learning economies: processing more transactions at higher intelligence per transaction. The firm that learns fastest wins.

Network Effects: The Value of Connection

A **network effect** occurs when the value of a service to each user increases as the total number of users increases. The classic example is the telephone: a telephone alone is worthless. With two telephones, it has some value. With a million telephones, it is indispensable. The value is not in the device itself but in the network of other users.

Network effects create natural monopolies. A social network with one million users is valuable. A competitor with one hundred thousand users is much less valuable—not because its technology is worse, but because its network is smaller. Users have no incentive to switch. The incumbent's advantage grows with its user base.

Direct vs. Indirect Network Effects

Direct network effects occur when value increases directly with the number of users of the same service. Messaging platforms (WhatsApp, WeChat), social networks (Facebook, LinkedIn), and marketplaces (eBay, Craigslist) exhibit direct effects. More buyers attract more sellers. More sellers attract more buyers. The cycle feeds itself.

Indirect network effects occur when value increases because more users of one service increase the supply of complementary goods or services. A gaming console becomes more valuable as more game developers write titles for it—not because there are more console owners directly, but because the installed base attracts developers, whose games attract more owners. This is cross-side network effect, common in platforms with distinct user groups.

How AI Amplifies Network Effects

In traditional digital businesses, network effects are powerful but passive. A larger network is more valuable, but the nature of that value is largely static. Facebook in 2010 was valuable because your friends were there. The algorithms that surfaced content were basic.

AI transforms network effects from passive to **active**. The larger network does not just contain more connections. It generates more data. And that data feeds the AI Factory, which uses it to improve the experience for every user individually.

Consider Netflix. A traditional network effect would be: more subscribers make Netflix more valuable because there are more people to discuss shows with. That effect exists but is weak. The real AI-amplified effect is: more subscribers generate more viewing data (what they watch, when they pause, what they search for). That data trains better recommendation models. Better recommendations improve retention and engagement for all subscribers, including the ones who joined yesterday. The new subscriber benefits not just from the size of the network but from the cumulative learning of everyone who came before.

This is the **hub dynamic**: a few dominant firms control the majority of interactions within an ecosystem because their AI-powered platforms learn from the collective behavior of the entire network. A new entrant cannot match the incumbent's intelligence because it cannot match the incumbent's data volume. The data is the moat.

Learning Effects: The Advantage of Experience

A **learning effect** occurs when a firm becomes more efficient at producing its output as it gains cumulative experience. In manufacturing, the learning curve is well documented: each doubling of cumulative production reduces unit costs by a predictable percentage (often 10-30%).

In the AI age, learning effects are not about physical production. They are about **decision quality**. Each transaction the AI Factory processes—each loan application, each recommendation request, each fraud check—becomes a training example for future transactions. The model improves continuously. The 100,000th prediction is more accurate than the 10,000th, which is more accurate than the 1,000th.

This is fundamentally different from traditional learning effects. In manufacturing, learning comes from human process improvement: workers discover faster methods, managers reorganize workflows, engineers redesign tools. This learning is slow, expensive, and hard to transfer. It happens through meetings and memos.

In the AI Factory, learning is **automatic and instantaneous**. The model does not hold a retrospective. It does not write a report. It updates its parameters based on the latest data, often in real time. Learning is not a separate activity; it is a byproduct of normal operations. Every transaction makes the next transaction smarter.

The Marginal Cost Collapse

The combination of network effects and learning effects produces a startling economic outcome: **the marginal cost of decision-making approaches zero**.

In a traditional bank, the cost of underwriting a loan includes the loan officer's salary, benefits, and overhead, divided by the number of loans they process. This cost is roughly constant. Processing more loans requires hiring more loan officers.

In an AI-native lender, the marginal cost of underwriting an additional loan is the cost of compute and data transfer—fractions of a cent. The first loan cost millions in R&D. The billionth loan costs almost nothing. The average cost drops continuously as volume increases, but the marginal cost drops to near-zero almost immediately.

This collapse of marginal cost has two strategic implications.

First, **scale becomes a weapon**. A firm that has already invested in building the AI Factory can serve additional customers at negligible cost. It can offer services that would be uneconomical for a smaller firm. It can enter adjacent markets by retargeting its existing models. It can outspend competitors on acquisition because it knows that the lifetime value of a new customer includes the data they generate, not just the revenue they bring.

Second, **pricing can decouple from cost**. When marginal cost is near-zero, any positive price generates contribution margin. The firm can price discriminatorily—charging different customers different prices based on their willingness to pay—without

worrying about covering variable costs. This enables strategies—freemium, subsidized entry, loss-leading—that traditional firms cannot match.

The Virtuous Data Cycle in Action

The virtuous data cycle is the fusion of network effects and learning effects into a single reinforcing loop. The diagram below illustrates the cycle:

Each turn of the cycle strengthens the firm's position. More users generate more data. More data produces better models. Better models create a better product. A better product attracts more users. The cycle spins faster as it grows.

Case Study: Waze

Waze, the navigation app acquired by Google, exemplifies the virtuous data cycle. Waze users share real-time traffic data: speed, location, accidents, police presence. More users mean more data. More data means more accurate traffic predictions and faster route recommendations. Better recommendations attract more users. A driver who is not on Waze receives no benefit from the network. A driver who joins Waze benefits from every other driver's data.

But Waze adds an AI layer. The traffic predictions are not just crowd-sourced; they are modeled. The system learns patterns: which roads clog at which times, how incidents propagate through the network, which reroutes actually save time. A new user in a city with many existing users immediately benefits from years of cumulative learning. The data moat is nearly unassailable. A competitor would need to build a comparable user base from scratch—but without the accurate predictions that would attract users in the first place.

Case Study: Ant Financial

Ant Financial, introduced in Chapter 2, demonstrates the virtuous data cycle in financial services. Each loan application generates data: the borrower's characteristics, the loan terms, the repayment outcome. More loans produce more data. More data produces better credit models. Better models enable Ant to approve loans that traditional banks would reject—borrowers with thin credit files, small business owners without formal financial statements. These previously unserved borrowers become loyal customers, generating more data. The cycle spins.

Traditional banks cannot compete because they lack the data. A bank that tries to copy Ant's underwriting model would have to train it on its own historical loan data. But that data reflects the bank's conservative underwriting—it contains few examples of the thin-file borrowers Ant serves. The model would not generalize. The bank would need to lend to risky borrowers to generate data, but without a good model to assess risk, it would take unacceptable losses. The data moat is insurmountable.

Winner-Take-Most: The New Market Structure

The virtuous data cycle does not always produce a pure winner-take-all market. But it reliably produces **winner-take-most** dynamics: a small number of dominant firms control the vast majority of market value, with a long tail of niche players serving the edges.

Why not pure winner-take-all? Because data has diminishing returns beyond a point. A model trained on one billion transactions is better than a model trained on one million. But the incremental improvement from one billion to ten billion is smaller. At some scale, additional data yields negligible gains. A focused competitor with a differentiated dataset—specialized to a particular geography, customer segment, or use case—can match the incumbent's model quality for that niche.

Moreover, network effects have geographic and cultural boundaries. WhatsApp dominates messaging in many countries, but WeChat dominates China, Line dominates Japan, and KakaoTalk dominates Korea. Each network's value is concentrated within a linguistic or regulatory boundary.

The strategic implication is not that only one firm survives. It is that **the window for competition is narrow**. A firm that establishes a virtuous data cycle in a market before competitors do will be extraordinarily difficult to dislodge. The second mover faces not just a product gap but a data gap. And data gaps compound over time.

Escaping the Cycle: When Challengers Win

Incumbents with virtuous data cycles can seem invincible. But challengers do sometimes win. How?

Discontinuous innovation: A challenger introduces a product architecture so different that the incumbent's data advantage becomes irrelevant. The incumbent's models are optimized for the old paradigm. The challenger starts fresh but with a superior approach. This is what Tesla did to incumbent automakers: their data on internal combustion engines was useless for training self-driving electric vehicles.

New data sources: A challenger gains access to a proprietary dataset that the incumbent cannot replicate. This could be exclusive access to a new sensor network, a partnership with a unique data provider, or a regulatory change that opens new data flows. The challenger's models may be initially weaker, but they learn from data the incumbent cannot see.

Privacy-constrained switching: Users may refuse to join the incumbent's network due to privacy concerns. If the incumbent's data advantage relies on collecting sensitive information, a challenger that offers strong privacy guarantees—even at the cost of weaker models—can attract users who value privacy over performance. This is the bet that Apple makes with its on-device processing and differential privacy.

Regulatory intervention: Antitrust regulators may force incumbents to share data, interoperate with competitors, or divest parts of their business. The European Union's Digital Markets Act and similar proposals in other jurisdictions aim to prevent the most extreme winner-take-most outcomes by mandating data portability and interoperability.

From Virtuous Cycle to Strategic Vulnerability

The virtuous data cycle is a source of strength, but it is also a source of vulnerability. The same dynamics that protect an incumbent can blind it.

Overfitting to the past: A model trained on historical data learns the patterns of the past. If the world changes—a pandemic, a new regulation, a shift in consumer preferences—the incumbent's models may become systematically wrong. The incumbent cannot easily retrain on data that does not yet exist. Challengers, with less historical baggage, may adapt faster.

Exploration vs. exploitation: The virtuous data cycle optimizes for exploitation: doing more of what has worked in the past. It systematically underinvests in exploration: trying things that might fail but might also discover new opportunities. An incumbent that perfects its existing business may miss the next business entirely.

Data ossification: As the cycle spins, the data that drives it becomes increasingly self-referential. The recommendation engine shows users what they have liked before, so users click on what they have liked before, so the engine learns to show more of the same. The system optimizes for short-term engagement at the expense of long-term discovery. Challengers that prioritize exploration over exploitation can capture users who have grown bored with the incumbent's predictable offerings.

The Leadership Implication

The virtuous data cycle is not automatic. It requires deliberate design. Leaders must ask:

- What is the data loop in our business? What data do we generate, and how does it improve our product?
- How do we accelerate the cycle? What would increase the rate of data generation, model improvement, or user acquisition?

- What prevents competitors from entering our cycle? What is our data moat?
- What could break our cycle? Where are we vulnerable to discontinuous innovation, new data sources, or regulatory change?

These are not technical questions. They are strategic questions about market structure, competitive dynamics, and long-term positioning. The AI Factory provides the engine. The virtuous data cycle provides the fuel. But leaders must steer.

From Amplification to Transformation

In Chapter 8, we turn from market dynamics to human dynamics. The virtuous data cycle creates enormous value—but that value is not distributed evenly. Some workers find their productivity amplified; others find their roles rebalanced; still others find themselves vulnerable, their skills rendered obsolete by the very intelligence they helped generate.

Effect Type	Mechanism	Resulting Advantage
Network Effects	Value increases with user base size	High barriers to entry, "winner-take-all"
Learning Effects	Algorithms improve with transaction volume	Superior precision, lower operational costs
Scale Effects	Fixed costs are spread over billions of units	Unmatched price competitiveness
Scope Effects	Data from one domain improves another	Rapid entry into adjacent industries

A circular diagram with five nodes connected by arrows:

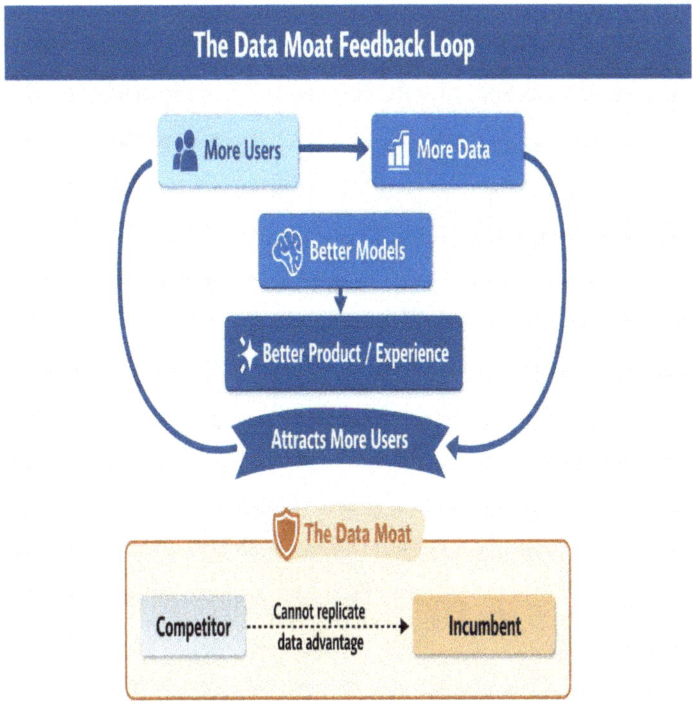

Figure 7: The Virtuous Data Cycle

Chapter 8

Strategic Collisions: Competitive Dynamics in the Era of Hub Firms

The Asymmetric Battlefield

For most of industrial history, competition followed predictable patterns. Firms competed within industry boundaries. A bank competed with other banks. A retailer competed with other retailers. A hospital competed with other hospitals. The battleground was familiar, the rules were understood, and the victors were determined by scale, efficiency, and capital.

That era is over.

Today, a software company can become a bank without building a single branch. A logistics company can become a retailer without owning a single store. A search engine can become a transportation network without owning a single vehicle. The boundaries that once defined industries have dissolved, and in their place is a single, continuous battlefield where digital-native firms collide with analog incumbants—and where the analog firms are losing.

This chapter examines these **strategic collisions**: the moments when an AI-centric firm enters a traditional industry and fundamentally reshapes its competitive landscape. We will explore why digital firms win, how hub firms concentrate power, and what incumbents must do to survive.

The Anatomy of a Collision

A strategic collision occurs when a firm built on the AI Factory architecture—data pipeline, algorithmic engine, experimentation platform, digital backbone—enters an industry dominated by firms built on the traditional operating model of human hierarchy and manual workflows.

The collision is asymmetric because the two types of firms operate under fundamentally different constraints.

The Traditional Firm's Constraints

Traditional firms are optimized for a world of scarce information, expensive communication, and slow change. Their operating model imposes four constraints that digital firms do not share:

Geographic constraint: A traditional bank must build branches to serve customers. Each branch requires real estate, staff, security, and regulatory approval. Expanding to a new city takes months or years. A digital bank serves any customer with an internet connection. Its expansion constraint is marketing spend and server capacity, not physical presence.

Capacity constraint: A traditional retailer's growth is limited by warehouse space, trucking capacity, and store shelf footage. Expanding requires capital investment in physical assets. A digital retailer's growth is limited by algorithm accuracy and server throughput. The marginal cost of an additional transaction approaches zero.

Information constraint: A traditional firm's decisions are based on sampled, delayed, and aggregated data. Monthly reports. Quarterly reviews. Annual planning. By the time information reaches decision-makers, it is stale. A digital firm's decisions are based on real-time, transaction-level data. The algorithm knows what happened one second ago, not one month ago.

Coordination constraint: A traditional firm's response to market change requires aligning dozens of managers across multiple departments. Decisions must be communicated, interpreted, and executed through layers of hierarchy. A digital firm's response requires updating a model and redeploying a service. The change propagates instantly.

The Digital Firm's Freedoms

Digital firms built on the AI Factory architecture enjoy the inverse of these constraints:

Freedom from geography: The cloud has no location. A digital firm serves customers wherever they are, using the same infrastructure, the same models, and the same teams. International expansion is a configuration change, not a capital project.

Freedom from capacity: Elastic compute means the firm never runs out of processing power. Demand spikes are absorbed automatically. The firm pays only for what it uses. There is no idle capacity and no capacity shortage.

Freedom from information latency: Real-time data pipelines mean the firm knows what is happening now. Models retrain continuously. Decisions are made in milliseconds, not days. The firm operates at the speed of light, not the speed of meetings.

Freedom from coordination overhead: APIs replace managers. Services communicate through well-defined interfaces, not through email chains. Changes deploy independently. The organization does not need to align because the architecture does not require alignment.

When a firm with these freedoms competes against a firm without them, the outcome is not in doubt. The digital firm will be faster, cheaper, and smarter. The only questions are how long the incumbent survives and what form its eventual decline takes.

Collisions in Practice

Retail: Amazon vs. Walmart

The most documented strategic collision is Amazon versus Walmart. Walmart was the undisputed king of retail efficiency. Its supply chain, inventory management, and logistics were the envy of the world. It had scale, capital, and decades of operational expertise.

But Walmart was built for a world of physical stores. Its operating model assumed that customers would come to its locations. Its information flowed weekly. Its decisions were made by managers who had worked in retail for thirty years.

Amazon was built for a different world. Its operating model assumed that customers wanted everything delivered to their doorsteps. Its information flowed in real time. Its decisions were made by algorithms that had learned from billions of previous transactions.

The collision played out exactly as the asymmetric constraints predicted. Amazon offered selection that Walmart could not match—not because Walmart lacked access to products, but because a physical store has finite shelf space. Amazon offered prices that Walmart could not beat—not because Walmart was inefficient, but because Amazon's cost structure had near-zero marginal cost for many categories. Amazon offered convenience that Walmart could not provide—not because Walmart's employees were lazy, but because driving to a store and walking the aisles takes time that delivery eliminates.

Walmart has survived by investing massively in its own AI capabilities: online ordering, curbside pickup, automated warehouses. But it has done so as a follower, not a leader. The collision permanently shifted the center of gravity in retail. Amazon set the new standard; Walmart races to meet it.

Finance: Ant Financial vs. Traditional Banking

The collision in finance is even more stark. Traditional banks are built on branch networks, human loan officers, and legacy IT systems. Their cost structures are fixed and high. Their decision-making is slow and inconsistent.

Ant Financial, as we have seen, is built on the AI Factory. No branches. No human loan officers. No legacy systems. Just data, algorithms, and the virtuous data cycle.

The collision produced an extraordinary outcome: Ant could serve customers that traditional banks considered unprofitable. A small business owner with no credit history, no collateral, and no formal financial statements could get a loan in three minutes. The algorithm did not need the documents that a human loan officer would demand. It found signals in transaction data, payment patterns, and social connections.

Traditional banks could not respond because they lacked the data. They had never served these customers, so they had no historical data to train models. They could not acquire the data without serving the customers, but they could not serve the customers without models to assess risk. The collision created a chicken-and-egg problem that Ant had already solved.

Healthcare: The Coming Collision

Healthcare is the next frontier. The industry remains dominated by traditional operating models: paper records, manual diagnosis, fragmented data. Decisions that could be made by algorithms are still made by humans with inconsistent training and incomplete information.

Digital firms are entering. Google's DeepMind is developing diagnostic algorithms that match or exceed human specialists in ophthalmology, radiology, and pathology. Flatiron Health is aggregating oncology data to personalize cancer treatment. Teladoc is delivering remote care that bypasses the traditional clinic visit.

The collision in healthcare will be slower than in retail or finance because regulation, patient safety, and professional licensure create barriers. But it will come. And when it does, the same asymmetric dynamics will apply. The digital firm will have more data, better models, and lower costs. The traditional hospital system will be constrained by geography, capacity, information latency, and coordination overhead.

Hub Firms: The Architects of the New Economy

The strategic collisions described above are not isolated events. They are symptoms of a deeper structural transformation: the emergence of **hub firms** that provide the infrastructure and platforms for the entire economy.

Hub firms—Amazon, Microsoft, Google, and to a lesser extent Apple, Meta, and Alibaba—started as competitors in specific markets. But they have evolved into something different. They are the firms that own the horizontal layers upon which other businesses depend.

The Three Layers of Hub Firm Control

Hub firms exert power through three interconnected layers:

Cloud infrastructure: Amazon Web Services, Microsoft Azure, and Google Cloud Platform provide the compute, storage, and networking that power the AI Factory for millions of other firms. A startup building an AI-native business does not build its own data center. It rents from a hub firm. This gives hub firms unprecedented visibility into the activity of the entire economy—and the ability to extract rents from every transaction.

Data ecosystems: Hub firms aggregate data across millions of users and billions of interactions. Google sees search queries. Amazon sees purchase behavior. Meta sees social connections.

These datasets are proprietary and immense. No competitor can replicate them. And because the virtuous data cycle amplifies advantage, the gap between hub firms and everyone else widens over time.

AI platforms: Hub firms are building the foundational models that other firms fine-tune and deploy. OpenAI (backed by Microsoft) provides GPT models that thousands of companies use as the basis for their own products. Google provides Gemini. Amazon provides Bedrock. These platforms become the operating system for the AI age. The hub firm that dominates the platform layer sets the rules for everyone who builds on top of it.

The Rules of the Game

Hub firms do not just compete in markets. They shape markets. They set the terms on which other firms participate. They decide which data is accessible, which APIs are available, and which behaviors are rewarded.

This is a new form of market power. In the industrial age, dominant firms controlled supply chains. They could dictate terms to suppliers because suppliers had few alternative buyers. In the AI age, hub firms control data flows and compute access. They can dictate terms to downstream firms because those firms cannot build their own cloud, cannot replicate the hub's data, and cannot train foundation models from scratch.

The result is an economy that is simultaneously more dynamic and more concentrated. New firms can launch quickly and scale globally—but they launch on hub infrastructure, within hub ecosystems, subject to hub rules. The barriers to starting a business have fallen. The barriers to independent business have risen.

Strategic Implications for Incumbents

For traditional incumbents facing collision from digital natives and hub firms, the path forward is narrow but not impossible. Three strategies have emerged.

Strategy One: Become a Hub Firm

A tiny number of incumbents can attempt to become hub firms themselves. Microsoft transformed from a software vendor to a cloud hub. Amazon transformed from a retailer to a cloud and logistics hub. These transformations required extraordinary investment, visionary leadership, and a willingness to cannibalize existing businesses.

Most incumbents cannot follow this path. The window has closed. Hub positions are locked in by virtuous data cycles and massive capital requirements. A traditional bank cannot become a cloud provider. A traditional retailer cannot become a foundation model lab. The time to make that bet was a decade ago.

Strategy Two: Niche Within a Hub Ecosystem

A more realistic strategy is to accept the hub firm's dominance at the horizontal layer while building deep vertical expertise on top. A healthcare provider cannot beat Google at cloud infrastructure. It can build the world's best AI-powered oncology service using Google's infrastructure.

This strategy requires **strategic humility**: acknowledging where you cannot compete and focusing your scarce resources where you can win. The niche firm becomes a complementor, not a competitor, to the hub. It accepts that the hub will capture some of the value—but captures enough value for itself to thrive.

The risk is that the hub firm eventually enters your niche. Amazon started as a book retailer, then became a general retailer, then became a logistics provider, then became a cloud provider. Hub firms expand relentlessly. A complementor today may be a competitor tomorrow.

Strategy Three: Differentiate on Non-Digital Assets

Some incumbents survive by leveraging assets that digital firms cannot easily replicate: physical footprint, regulatory relationships, brand trust, human expertise.

A regional bank with deep relationships in a local community may survive against Ant Financial because small business owners trust the local loan officer in a way they do not trust an algorithm. A hospital system with world-class specialists may survive against diagnostic AI because patients want a human doctor to deliver bad news. A luxury retailer with exclusive brand relationships may survive against Amazon because wealthy customers value the in-person experience.

But these advantages erode. Trust can be built digitally. Human expertise can be augmented by AI. Brand relationships can be replicated. The non-digital moat is a delaying tactic, not a permanent defense. Incumbents that rely on it without simultaneously building their own AI capabilities will eventually be overtaken.

The Social Implications of Hub Dominance

The rise of hub firms and the acceleration of strategic collisions have social implications that extend beyond market competition.

Labor markets: Hub firms concentrate wealth and employment in a small number of high-skill, high-wage roles. The middle-skill jobs that sustained the industrial middle class—bank tellers, retail managers, logistics coordinators—are precisely the roles most vulnerable to AI automation. Chapter 9 examines this transformation in detail.

Geographic inequality: Hub firms cluster in a handful of cities: San Francisco, Seattle, New York, Boston. The economic benefits of the AI revolution accrue to these places. Regions that depended on traditional industries—manufacturing, retail, finance—face decline without obvious paths to recovery.

Market power and democracy: Hub firms control critical infrastructure. When a few companies decide what information is visible, what products are available, and what services are accessible, they wield a form of power that rivals governments. The regulatory response to this power is still evolving—and is likely to be one of the defining political battles of the coming decade.

From Collision to Transformation

Strategic collisions are not one-time events. They are ongoing processes that reshape industries from the inside out. Every collision changes the terrain, making future collisions easier for digital firms and harder for incumbents.

In Chapter 9, we turn from the fate of firms to the fate of workers. The AI Factory does not just compete with traditional organizations. It transforms the nature of work itself. Some roles are amplified. Some are rebalanced. Some are enabled. And some —a significant and painful category—are rendered vulnerable.

The collision between digital and analog plays out not only in boardrooms and balance sheets but in the daily lives of millions of workers. How organizations manage this human transformation will determine not only their own success but the social legitimacy of the AI age itself.

Industry Sector	Traditional Player Approach	AI Hub Firm Approach
Retail	Inventory-led, seasonal planning	Demand-led, real-time algorithmic replenishment
Banking	Human-led credit committees	Automated, real-time credit scoring
Logistics	Route planning based on experience	Dynamically optimized routing via AI
Media	Programming for the "average" viewer	Hyper-personalized content streams

Figure 8: The Asymmetric Collision

A two-column comparison:

Dimension	Traditional Incumbent	Digital Native
Geographic constraint	Physical presence required	Serves anyone with internet
Capacity constraint	Capital-intensive assets	Elastic cloud compute
Information latency	Monthly reports	Real-time data
Coordination overhead	Hierarchical approvals	APIs and automation
Marginal cost	Positive constant	Approaches zero
Learning speed	Quarterly reviews	Continuous

Below the table, a time-series chart showing "Market Share Over Time" — a declining line for the incumbent and a rising line for the digital native.

Caption: When a digital native collides with a traditional incumbent, the outcome is determined not by effort but by architecture.

Chapter 9

The Reshaped Workforce: Amplified, Rebalanced, and Enabled Roles

Beyond the Replacement Narrative

For as long as artificial intelligence has existed as a concept, it has been accompanied by a shadow: the fear of mass unemployment. From the Luddites smashing looms in 19th-century England to the anxious headlines about ChatGPT replacing writers and coders, the dominant narrative has been one of replacement. Machines take jobs. Humans are left behind.

This narrative is not wrong, but it is incomplete. Yes, some jobs will be eliminated. Yes, some workers will be displaced. But the more profound story is one of reshaping. AI does not simply replace what humans do. It changes what humans do, shifting the distribution of tasks, the premium on different skills, and the very structure of work.

This chapter offers a framework for understanding that reshaping. We identify four categories into which roles fall as the AI Factory matures: **Amplified**, **Rebalanced**, **Enabled**, and **Vulnerable**. For each category, we describe the nature of the transformation, the implications for workers and organizations, and the strategic choices leaders must make.

The stakes are high. Research indicates that over 50% of jobs will be materially affected by AI within the next few years. The organizations that manage this transition well will gain access to talent, build trust, and avoid the social disruption that has accompanied past technological revolutions. The organizations that manage it poorly will face resistance, attrition, and reputational damage.

The Four Categories of Work

The following table summarizes the four categories:

Category	Relationship to AI	Skill Premium	Organizational Action
Amplified	AI augments human judgment	Domain expertise, creativity, synthesis	Upskill to leverage AI tools
Rebalanced	Task distribution shifts	Empathy, ethics, complex reasoning	Redesign roles and incentives
Enabled	Roles that did not exist before AI	Hybrid (technical + domain)	Recruit and develop new capabilities
Vulnerable	AI substitutes for human labor	Routine pattern recognition	Reskill, redeploy, or manage transition

No role is permanently fixed in a single category. A role that is Amplified today may become Rebalanced tomorrow as AI capabilities advance. A role that is Vulnerable today may be

Enabled if the organization invests in reskilling. The categories are diagnostic tools, not destiny.

Amplified Roles: Humans Augmented by AI

In **Amplified** roles, AI acts as a cognitive exoskeleton. The human remains the decision-maker, the creative force, the accountable party. But AI handles the routine subtasks that once consumed the majority of time and attention.

How Amplification Works

Consider the work of an architect. Traditionally, an architect conceives a design, drafts plans, calculates loads, checks building codes, and revises based on feedback. The creative conception is the highest-value activity, but it consumes a small fraction of total time. The majority is drafting, calculating, and checking—necessary but lower-value.

With AI tools, the architect can generate dozens of design variations from a high-level prompt. The AI drafts floor plans, calculates structural loads, and flags code violations. The architect reviews, selects, refines, and synthesizes. The AI handles the generation; the human handles the judgment. The architect's output multiplies. The architect's value—the creative synthesis that only a human can provide—becomes a larger share of the total.

The same pattern appears in software development. An AI pair programmer generates boilerplate, writes tests, and suggests completions. The human developer reviews the code, understands the system architecture, and ensures that the components fit together correctly. The developer's role shifts from writing code to orchestrating code—a higher-level, more valuable activity.

The Skill Premium in Amplified Roles

Amplification changes which skills are valuable. Routine execution skills—the ability to draft a floor plan quickly, the ability to write boilerplate code accurately—become less valuable because AI does them better. Higher-order skills become more valuable:

•**Domain expertise**: You cannot judge what the AI generates unless you know what good looks like. The amplified architect needs deep knowledge of design principles, materials, and building codes. The amplified developer needs deep understanding of system architecture and software design patterns.
•**Creative synthesis**: AI generates variations. Humans select and combine. The ability to see connections across disparate ideas, to synthesize multiple constraints into a coherent whole, becomes the core of value creation.
•**Problem formulation**: AI is good at answering questions. Humans must ask the right questions. The amplified role requires the ability to break down ambiguous problems into tasks that AI can help solve.
•**Organizational Implications**

Organizations with amplified roles must invest in **upskilling**. The tools change faster than the underlying expertise. An architect who learned drafting software a decade ago must learn prompt engineering today. A developer who mastered one IDE must master AI pair programming.

Upskilling is not a one-time training event. It is a continuous process. The organizations that succeed build learning into the workflow: lunch-and-learns, internal communities of practice, dedicated time for experimentation. They treat AI literacy as a core competency, not a nice-to-have.

Rebalanced Roles: The Shifting Center of Gravity

In **Rebalanced** roles, the distribution of tasks shifts dramatically. Some tasks that were once core become automated. Other tasks that were once peripheral become central. The role does not disappear, but its center of gravity moves.

The Managerial Rebalancing

The most significant rebalancing is happening in management. The traditional manager's role was built on information asymmetry. Subordinates knew what they were doing; managers aggregated that information and reported upward. The manager's value was in oversight: monitoring progress, catching errors, coordinating across teams.

AI collapses the information asymmetry. A real-time dashboard shows what every team is working on, how each project is progressing, and where bottlenecks are emerging. The manager no longer needs to ask for status updates. The system provides them automatically.

What, then, does a manager do? The role rebalances from oversight to **coaching and orchestration**. The manager's value shifts to:

•**Developing people**: Coaching team members on their skills, careers, and challenges. AI cannot build trust, provide emotional support, or see potential that is not yet realized.
•**Navigating ambiguity**: When the problem is not well-defined, when the data is conflicting, when the stakeholders disagree—these are the situations where human judgment is essential. AI can provide inputs, but humans must make the call.
•**Building culture**: Creating the shared norms, values, and practices that enable teams to work together effectively. Culture is not a dataset. It is a living, negotiated reality.

This rebalancing is challenging for managers who rose through the ranks on their ability to monitor and report. Their skills are suddenly less relevant. The organizations that succeed will invest in **retraining managers** for the coaching role—and will be honest with those who cannot make the transition.

The Clinical Rebalancing

Healthcare offers another example of rebalancing. A radiologist's traditional role centered on pattern recognition: reviewing images, identifying abnormalities, making diagnoses. AI now matches or exceeds human performance on many of these pattern-recognition tasks.

The radiologist's role rebalances. The AI handles the initial read, flagging suspicious areas and suggesting diagnoses. The radiologist focuses on the ambiguous cases, integrates the imaging findings with the patient's history and symptoms, and communicates the results to the patient and care team. The role shifts from pattern recognizer to clinical integrator and communicator.

This rebalancing requires different training. Radiology residencies traditionally emphasized visual perception and anatomy. The rebalanced role requires communication skills, systems thinking, and the ability to manage AI as a teammate. Medical education is only beginning to adapt.

The Skill Premium in Rebalanced Roles

Rebalanced roles place a premium on distinctly human skills that AI cannot replicate:

- **Empathy**: Understanding another person's emotional state and responding appropriately. This is essential in management, healthcare, education, and any role involving human relationships.
- **Ethical judgment**: Navigating trade-offs between competing values. AI can optimize for a stated objective, but it cannot decide what the objective should be. That is a human responsibility.
- **Complex social reasoning**: Understanding organizational politics, building coalitions, managing stakeholders. These are the skills of influence and negotiation, and they remain firmly in the human domain.

Organizational Implications

Organizations with rebalanced roles must **redesign role definitions, incentive systems, and career paths**. The person who excelled as a traditional manager may fail as a coaching manager. The radiologist who loved pattern recognition may be unhappy in a role that emphasizes patient communication.

Redesign is not simply adding "AI literacy" to job descriptions. It is fundamentally rethinking what the role exists to do. This is uncomfortable work because it challenges assumptions that have been embedded in organizational structures for decades. But it is necessary work. The old definitions no longer fit.

Enabled Roles: New Categories of Work

Enabled roles are those that did not exist before AI. They are not reshaped from previous roles; they are entirely new. They emerge because AI creates capabilities that did not previously exist—and those capabilities require human oversight, direction, and governance

Model Trainers and Curators

Machine learning models require training data. That data must be labeled, cleaned, and curated. The humans who do this work—sometimes called data labelers, annotation specialists, or training data curators—are an emerging workforce. They may have domain expertise (medical professionals labeling scans) or specialized annotation skills (linguists labeling sentiment). Their work is essential; without high-quality labels, models do not learn.

The paradox of this role is that it is simultaneously enabled by AI and vulnerable to automation. As models become more sophisticated, they can generate their own training data or learn from weaker supervision. Some labeling jobs will be automated. Others will evolve into quality assurance roles, where humans validate and correct model-generated labels.

Prompt Engineers

Large language models respond to prompts. The same model can produce brilliant analysis or incoherent nonsense depending on how it is prompted. **Prompt engineering**—the craft of designing inputs to elicit desired outputs from generative AI—has emerged as a new discipline.

Prompt engineers understand the model's capabilities and failure modes. They know how to structure prompts to reduce hallucination, how to chain prompts for complex tasks, and how to evaluate model outputs. The role sits at the intersection of linguistics, psychology, and software engineering. It did not exist three years ago. It is now a sought-after skill.

Ethical Governance Officers

As AI systems make consequential decisions—approving loans, diagnosing diseases, recommending prison sentences—the need for governance grows. **Ethical governance officers** design and operate the systems that monitor AI for bias, fairness, safety, and compliance.

This role requires a rare combination of skills: technical understanding of machine learning, legal and regulatory knowledge, and philosophical grounding in ethics. The ethical governance officer does not merely audit models after they are built. They design the processes that ensure models are built responsibly from the start. They define the metrics for fairness, the thresholds for safety, and the procedures for redress when AI systems cause harm.

AI Operations Engineers

The AI Factory must run continuously. Models must be deployed, monitored, retrained, and retired. **AI operations (AIOps) engineers** manage this lifecycle. They build the infrastructure for continuous integration and deployment of models. They monitor prediction latency, data drift, and model performance. They roll back models that degrade. They scale serving infrastructure to meet demand.

This role blends software engineering, data engineering, and machine learning. It is the operational backbone of the mature AI Factory. And it is in desperately short supply. The organizations that invest in building AI Ops capabilities will have a significant advantage over those that treat model deployment as an afterthought.

The Skill Premium in Enabled Roles

Enabled roles demand **hybrid skills**. They require technical fluency without necessarily requiring full-stack engineering. They require domain knowledge without necessarily requiring deep specialization. The prompt engineer needs to understand language and logic, but does not need to write production code. The ethical governance officer needs to understand bias metrics, but does not need to train foundation models.

This hybridity is challenging for traditional education and hiring systems. Universities train specialists. HR departments filter by narrow job titles. Enabled roles fall through the cracks. Organizations that succeed in hiring for these roles will need to broaden their definitions of qualifications, value demonstrated capability over credentials, and invest in internal training programs.

Vulnerable Categories: The Concentration of Displacement Risk

Not all roles are amplified, rebalanced, or enabled. Some are **vulnerable**—at high risk of displacement because AI can substitute for human labor entirely.

Characteristics of Vulnerable Roles

Vulnerable roles share three characteristics:

Standardization: The work follows predictable rules and procedures. There is a right way and a wrong way. Variation is a bug, not a feature.

Repeatability: The same task occurs many times with minor variations. The work does not require novel solutions to novel problems.

No required physical presence or complex interpersonal judgment: The work can be done entirely through a screen, or the physical components can be automated. The work does not require empathy, trust-building, or nuanced social reasoning.

Which Roles Are Most Vulnerable?

Research on AI labor displacement consistently identifies the following categories as highest risk:

Routine knowledge work: Data entry, document processing, basic accounting, invoice verification, appointment scheduling. These roles involve pattern recognition and rule application—exactly what supervised learning does best.

Customer service (tier one): Handling common inquiries, resetting passwords, checking account balances. These interactions are predictable and can be automated with chatbots and voice assistants. The remaining customer service roles will be rebalanced to handle complex exceptions, not routine inquiries.

Content generation (commodity): Writing basic news articles (earnings reports, sports summaries), creating simple marketing copy, generating standard legal documents. Generative AI produces passable output at near-zero marginal cost.

Translation (non-creative): Literal translation of documents where accuracy matters more than style. AI translation is already excellent for many language pairs and will continue to improve.

Manufacturing quality inspection: Visual inspection of products on assembly lines. Computer vision matches or exceeds human accuracy, works continuously, and never gets tired.

Manufacturing and Routine Professional Services

Two sectors face the highest concentration of displacement risk:

Manufacturing: The factory floor has been automating for decades. AI accelerates this trend by adding cognitive automation to physical automation. Robots that see, classify, and decide can replace humans in tasks that were previously too variable to automate. The jobs that remain will be rebalanced toward maintenance, troubleshooting, and exception handling.

Routine professional services: Accounting, legal document review, medical coding, loan underwriting, insurance claims processing. These are white-collar roles that involve standardized, repeatable cognitive work. They are as vulnerable as manufacturing jobs were thirty years ago. The difference is that the displacement will happen faster because software scales more quickly than robotics.

The Human Reality of Vulnerability

It is easy to write about vulnerable roles in the abstract. The human reality is brutal. Workers who have spent decades building skills find those skills devalued overnight. They face retraining at an age when learning is harder and employment gaps are more punishing. They carry mortgages, tuition bills, and healthcare costs. They are not abstract factors of production. They are people.

Organizations have a moral and strategic obligation to manage vulnerable labor with dignity. The moral obligation is obvious: workers who gave years of their lives to the organization deserve more than a severance check. The strategic obligation is less obvious but equally important: how an organization treats its displaced workers affects how remaining workers perceive the organization. Trust is hard to build and easy to destroy.

Managing the Transition: A Framework for Leaders

No organization can avoid workforce transformation. But organizations can choose how they manage it. The following principles guide effective transition management.

Principle One: Be Honest About Vulnerabilities

Pretending that AI will not affect certain roles is a disservice to workers. Leaders must be honest about which roles are vulnerable, which are changing, and which are growing. This honesty enables workers to plan, retrain, and make career decisions. It also builds trust, because workers are not naive—they see what is coming.

Principle Two: Invest in Reskilling, Not Just Severance

The cheapest option is to lay off vulnerable workers and hire new ones with different skills. The better option—for workers, for organizational culture, and often for the bottom line—is to reskill existing workers into amplified, rebalanced, or enabled roles.

Reskilling requires investment. It requires time away from production, dedicated learning resources, and patient managers who tolerate mistakes. But the return on investment is measured in retained institutional knowledge, maintained trust, and avoided severance costs. Many organizations underinvest in reskilling because the benefits are diffuse and the costs are immediate. Leaders must resist that short-term bias.

Principle Three: Redesign Roles Before Automating Them

The worst time to think about workforce implications is after the automation decision has been made. The best time is during role design. When planning to introduce AI into a process, ask: How does this change what the human does? What new skills will be required? Which current skills become obsolete? How will we support the transition?

Redesigning before automating enables proactive reskilling, honest communication, and smoother transitions. It also often reveals that full automation is not optimal—a human-AI hybrid may be more effective than either alone.

Principle Four: Measure Success Beyond Efficiency

If the only metric of AI success is headcount reduction, the organization will optimize for headcount reduction. Leaders must broaden the metrics to include: retention of institutional knowledge, successful reskilling completions, employee satisfaction, and speed of redeployment.

These metrics are harder to measure than "we reduced headcount by X%." But they matter. An organization that decimates its workforce to save costs will find that it has also decimated its culture, its trust, and its ability to attract talent in the future.

The Long Arc of Work

The reshaping of work is not a one-time event. It is an ongoing process that will accelerate as AI capabilities improve. Roles that are amplified today may become rebalanced next year and vulnerable in five years. The half-life of skills is shrinking.

This is terrifying. It is also an opportunity. The organizations that treat workforce transformation as a continuous discipline—constantly assessing roles, investing in reskilling, redesigning work—will build a competitive advantage in talent. They will attract workers who want to grow, not just collect a paycheck. They will retain workers who feel invested in.

	High Task Variability	Low Task Variability
High Judgment Required	**AMPLIFIED** (AI augments human; e.g., architect, doctor)	**REBALANCED** (Skills shift; e.g., manager, radiologist)
Low Judgment Required	**ENABLED** (New roles; e.g., prompt engineer, ethics officer)	**VULNERABLE** (High displacement risk; e.g., data entry, basic customer service)

Figure 9: The Four Categories of Work

Caption: Every role falls into one of four categories. The smart organization invests in moving roles up and to the

Chapter 10

The Human-Machine Synthesis: Orchestration & Judgment-Intensive Handoffs

Beyond the Binary

For decades, the conversation about AI and work has been trapped in a binary: man versus machine. Either machines replace humans, or humans resist machines. Either we automate fully, or we keep humans in the loop. Either we trust the algorithm, or we trust the expert.

This binary is a trap. The reality of the AI Factory is not replacement but **synthesis**. Humans and machines work together, each compensating for the other's weaknesses, each amplifying the other's strengths. The question is not "Who does the work?" but "How do we orchestrate the collaboration?"

This chapter explores that orchestration. We examine the operational reality of human-in-the-loop systems: how workflows are redesigned to combine human and AI capabilities, how judgment-intensive handoffs are managed when algorithms encounter ambiguity, and how organizations navigate the strategic trade-offs between full automation and human augmentation.

The synthesis is not easy. It requires rethinking processes that have existed for decades, building infrastructure that supports seamless handoffs, and training humans to work alongside algorithms that are simultaneously brilliant and brittle. But the organizations that master this synthesis will achieve what neither humans nor machines could accomplish alone: systems that are fast, scalable, accurate, and resilient.

Workflow Orchestration: Dividing the Cognitive Labor

The first task of human-machine synthesis is **workflow orchestration**: determining, for each step of a process, whether the task is better suited to a machine or a human—and then designing the handoffs between them.

What Machines Do Best

AI excels at tasks with the following characteristics:

•**Scale**: Processing millions of transactions, images, or documents in parallel.
•**Speed**: Making decisions in milliseconds, without fatigue or distraction.
•**Consistency**: Applying the same rules the same way every time, without variation due to mood, hunger, or distraction.
•**Pattern recognition**: Identifying subtle correlations in high-dimensional data that humans cannot perceive.
•**Repetition**: Performing the same task millions of times without degradation.

When the task requires these capabilities, machines should lead.

What Humans Do Best

Humans excel at tasks with the following characteristics:

•**Contextual judgment**: Understanding that a rule applies differently in different situations. The algorithm sees a transaction that matches a fraud pattern; the human sees that the customer just returned from vacation in a high-risk country. Context matters.

- **Creativity**: Generating novel solutions to novel problems. The algorithm has seen patterns in the training data; it cannot invent a new category.
- **Empathy**: Understanding and responding to emotional states. The algorithm can detect sentiment; it cannot genuinely care.
- **Moral reasoning**: Navigating trade-offs between competing values. The algorithm can optimize for a stated objective; it cannot decide what the objective should be.
- **Explanation**: Communicating decisions in terms that another human can understand and trust. The algorithm produces a prediction; the human produces a narrative.

When the task requires these capabilities, humans should lead.

The Orchestration Pattern

The mature human-machine synthesis follows a pattern:

1. **Machine handles the routine**. The AI processes the standard cases, the predictable transactions, the clear patterns. This is the vast majority of volume.
2. **Machine flags the ambiguous**. When the algorithm's confidence falls below a threshold, when the input is unusual, when the stakes are high—the system escalates.
3. **Human resolves the exception**. The human receives the case, reviews the machine's analysis, applies contextual judgment, and makes the final decision.
4. **Human feedback improves the machine**. The human's decision becomes a training label. The next time a similar case appears, the machine may handle it correctly.

This pattern is sometimes called a **human-in-the-loop** system. But that phrase is misleading because it suggests that humans are an occasional override to an otherwise autonomous system. In fact, the human and machine are co-equal partners, each doing what they do best, with handoffs happening continuously and seamlessly.

Judgment-Intensive Handoffs: The Critical Bridge

The most challenging moment in any human-machine synthesis is the **handoff**—the transition of a decision from algorithm to human. Handoffs are where systems fail. The algorithm may not recognize that it needs help. The human may receive insufficient context. The handoff may take too long, defeating the purpose of automation.

Judgment-intensive handoffs are those where the algorithm encounters a situation that exceeds its capabilities. These situations fall into three categories.

Category One: Low Confidence

The algorithm produces a prediction but with low confidence. A credit scoring model might be 99% confident for most applicants but only 60% confident for an applicant with an unusual income pattern. When confidence is low, the risk of error is high. The system should escalate to a human.

Low-confidence handoffs require a **confidence threshold**—a probability below which the algorithm defers. Setting this threshold involves trade-offs. A lower threshold keeps more decisions automated but increases error risk. A higher threshold defers more decisions to humans, reducing error risk but increasing cost and latency. The optimal threshold depends on the cost of error versus the cost of human review.

Category Two: Out-of-Distribution Input

The algorithm receives an input that is fundamentally different from its training data. A fraud detection model trained on consumer transactions receives a corporate transaction. A medical diagnostic model trained on adult patients receives a pediatric case. The algorithm may produce a high-confidence prediction, but that confidence is unwarranted because the input is outside its domain of competence.

Out-of-distribution detection is an active area of research. Simple methods include monitoring feature values for ranges not seen in training, or using anomaly detection models to flag unusual inputs. More sophisticated methods use uncertainty quantification to estimate when the model is operating in a regime it does not understand.

Category Three: Moral Ambiguity

The algorithm faces a decision with moral weight that cannot be reduced to optimization. A loan denial affects a family's ability to buy a home. A medical triage decision affects who receives scarce resources. A hiring algorithm's recommendation affects someone's career trajectory.

These decisions require **moral reasoning**—the ability to weigh competing values, to consider individual circumstances, to be accountable for outcomes. Current AI has no capacity for moral reasoning. It can optimize for fairness according to a defined metric, but it cannot decide what fairness means. These decisions must be escalated to humans.

Designing Effective Handoffs

Effective judgment-intensive handoffs require four design elements:

Clear escalation criteria: The system must know when to escalate. This requires defining confidence thresholds, out-of-distribution detectors, and moral flag conditions. These criteria must be calibrated carefully: too sensitive, and humans are overwhelmed with trivial cases; too insensitive, and costly errors slip through.

Rich context transmission: When a case escalates, the human must receive not just the raw input but the algorithm's analysis, its confidence, its reasoning (if interpretable), and the history of similar cases. The human should not have to rediscover what the algorithm already knows.

Low-latency handoff: The handoff must be fast. In a fraud detection system, a transaction cannot wait hours for human review. The system must route the case to an available human, present the context clearly, and capture the decision efficiently. This requires integrating human review into the same real-time infrastructure that serves automated decisions.

Closed feedback loop: The human's decision must flow back into the training data. The system learns from handoffs. Over time, cases that once required escalation may become routine enough for automation. The handoff criteria must be continuously recalibrated as the model improves.

Augmentation vs. Replacement: The Strategic Trade-Off

Organizations face a strategic choice for every process: **augment** humans with AI, or **replace** humans with AI. The choice has profound implications for cost, quality, resilience, and trust.

The Case for Replacement

Full automation offers the lowest marginal cost. Once the AI system is built and deployed, each additional transaction costs fractions of a cent. There is no human salary, no training, no turnover, no fatigue. The system runs 24/7/365. It scales infinitely.

Full automation also offers consistency. The algorithm applies the same rules to every case. There is no variation due to mood, bias, or distraction. For processes where consistency is paramount—fraud detection, credit scoring, quality inspection—automation can exceed human performance.

The case for replacement is strongest in **routine, high-volume, low-stakes** domains. A recommendation engine that shows the wrong product is annoying, not catastrophic. A spam filter that blocks a legitimate email is frustrating, not harmful.

The Case for Augmentation

Augmentation keeps humans in the loop, with AI handling routine subtasks and escalating ambiguity. The marginal cost is higher than full automation because human time is expensive. But augmentation offers three advantages that pure automation cannot match.

Quality: In non-routine domains, human-AI teams outperform either alone. The AI sees patterns the human would miss. The human applies context the AI cannot grasp. Together, they make better decisions than either could separately.

Resilience: AI systems are brittle. They fail gracefully only when they have been trained on failure modes. In novel situations—a pandemic disrupting consumer behavior, a new regulation changing the rules, an adversary actively trying to fool the system—pure automation can fail catastrophically. Humans adapt.

Trust: Many stakeholders—customers, regulators, employees—do not trust fully automated decisions, especially in high-stakes domains. A loan denial from an algorithm feels arbitrary and unaccountable. The same denial from a human who reviewed the algorithm's recommendation and applied judgment feels fairer, even if the outcome is identical. Augmentation preserves accountability.

The case for augmentation is strongest in **non-routine, variable, high-stakes** domains. Medical diagnosis, loan approval for non-standard applicants, legal judgment, hiring decisions—these are domains where the world is too complex for current AI to navigate alone, and where the cost of error is too high to accept without human oversight.

The False Binary

The augmentation-replacement binary is false in practice. Most processes are not purely one or the other. They are a **continuum**:

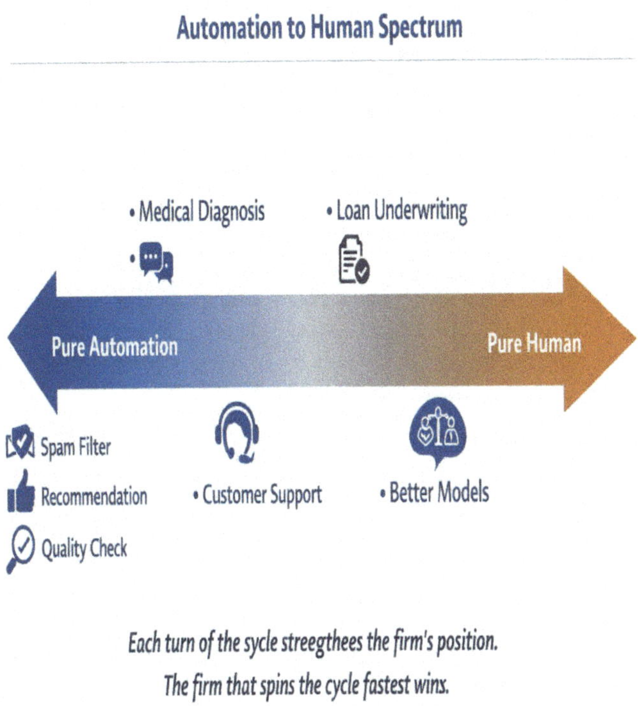

The optimal point on the continuum shifts over time. As AI capabilities improve, tasks that once required augmentation become automatable. As the cost of human review falls (through better tools and training), tasks that were once fully automated may benefit from augmentation.

The strategic discipline is not choosing a point on the continuum and staying there. It is continuously **re-evaluating** the frontier, retraining models, recalibrating handoff thresholds, and redesigning workflows as the relative capabilities of humans and machines change.

Human-in-the-Loop in Practice: Case Studies

Case Study: Autonomous Vehicles

Self-driving cars are the most complex human-machine synthesis deployed at scale. The vehicle's AI handles the routine: staying in lane, maintaining speed, following traffic signals. It handles the predictable: merging onto a highway, navigating a roundabout. But it encounters judgment-intensive handoffs constantly.

Consider a construction zone with ambiguous signage. The vehicle's perception system detects cones and barriers but cannot determine the correct path. The handoff: the system slows, alerts a remote human operator, presents the camera views and sensor data, and requests guidance. The operator reviews, provides a command ("take the left lane"), and the vehicle proceeds. The interaction takes seconds.

Consider a pedestrian who appears to be about to step into the street but hesitates. The vehicle must predict intent—a fundamentally ambiguous inference. The handoff: the system flags low confidence, reduces speed to safe level, and if the ambiguity persists, escalates to a human. But the human cannot respond instantly; the vehicle must make a fallback decision (stop) while awaiting guidance.

Autonomous vehicle companies have learned that handoffs must be **graceful**. The system cannot simply "give up" when it encounters ambiguity. It must have a safe default behavior, and it must request human help without requiring instantaneous response.

Case Study: Content Moderation

Content moderation at scale—deciding whether a piece of user-generated content violates platform policies—is impossible for humans alone. Billions of posts, images, and videos are uploaded daily. But it is also impossible for AI alone. The context matters: a violent image might be prohibited in one context (a threat) but acceptable in another (a news report about violence).

The synthesis: AI models perform the first pass. They flag obvious violations (child sexual abuse material, spam) with high confidence. They also flag ambiguous content—hate speech that depends on context, misinformation that references current events. These flags are routed to human moderators.

The human receives the content, the AI's analysis, and any relevant context (the poster's history, the discussion thread, current events). The human makes the final decision. That decision becomes a training label, improving the AI for future cases.

The challenge is human scale. Moderation is psychologically damaging work. Humans who review violent or abusive content experience trauma. The synthesis must protect moderators: limiting their exposure to the most disturbing content, providing mental health support, and rotating them through less intense tasks.

Case Study: Enterprise IT Help Desk

An enterprise IT help desk receives thousands of tickets per day: password resets, software installations, network connectivity issues. Most are routine. A few are complex.

The synthesis: A chatbot handles the routine. It authenticates the user, asks clarifying questions, and attempts automated resolution. For password resets, it can complete the entire flow without human involvement. For complex issues—"my custom reporting dashboard stopped working after the software update"—the chatbot recognizes its limitations and escalates.

The escalation creates a "warm handoff." The chatbot has already collected the user's identity, the problem description, and the troubleshooting steps attempted. The human agent receives this context, does not need to ask the user to repeat themselves, and can focus on solving the problem.

The synthesis reduces average resolution time from hours to minutes. The humans focus on the 20% of tickets that require judgment, not the 80% that are routine. The chatbot learns from each human resolution, gradually expanding the set of issues it can handle.

The Organizational Implications of Synthesis

Human-machine synthesis is not just a technical challenge. It is an organizational one.

New Roles for Humans

The humans in a synthesis system are not doing the same work they did before. They are doing new work:

- **Exception handlers**: Resolving the cases the algorithm could not handle. This requires judgment, pattern recognition across edge cases, and the ability to work efficiently with AI-generated context.
- **Trainers and labelers**: Producing the labeled data that improves the models. This requires domain expertise and attention to detail.
- **System monitors**: Watching dashboards for model drift, data pipeline failures, or unusual patterns of escalations. This requires vigilance and the ability to diagnose system-level issues.
- **Ethics reviewers**: Auditing decisions for bias, fairness, and compliance. This requires moral reasoning and regulatory knowledge.
- **New Skills for Managers**

Managers of human-machine systems need different skills than managers of traditional teams:

- **Calibrating handoffs**: Setting confidence thresholds, tuning escalation criteria, balancing automation rate against error rate.
- **Managing hybrid teams**: Leading groups where some "members" are algorithms with different capabilities and failure modes.
- **Measuring system performance**: Tracking not just human productivity but human-AI team outcomes, handoff latency, and closed-loop learning.
- **Maintaining human skills**: Ensuring that humans retain the judgment skills they need for exception handling, even as routine cases are automated away.

New Metrics for Success

Traditional metrics focus on either automation (cases per hour, cost per case) or human performance (accuracy, satisfaction). Synthesis requires metrics that capture the team:

- **Automation rate**: What percentage of cases are resolved without human involvement?
- **Handoff precision**: When the system escalates, was escalation appropriate? (Low false positives reduce human efficiency; low false negatives increase error risk.)
- **Human value-add**: When a human handles a case, do they improve on the algorithm's initial recommendation? (If humans always agree with the algorithm, they are not adding value.)
- **Learning rate**: How quickly does the system reduce its escalation rate over time as models improve from human feedback?
- **The Future of Synthesis**

The synthesis described in this chapter is the state of the art today. But it is not the final state. Three trends will reshape human-machine synthesis in the coming years.

Trend One: From Handoffs to Collaboration

Today's handoffs are discrete: the algorithm processes until it reaches an impasse, then escalates. The human resolves, and the algorithm continues. This is "human-in-the-loop" in its most basic form.

The future is **continuous collaboration**. The human and AI work together on the same problem in real time. The AI suggests, the human critiques. The human directs, the AI executes. The handoff is not a moment but a continuous dance. This is already emerging in creative tools (AI generates, human selects and refines) and will spread to decision-making domains.

Trend Two: From Exception Handling to Guided Exploration

Today's handoffs are reactive: the algorithm escalates when it is uncertain. The human responds to the algorithm's uncertainty.

The future is **proactive**: the human directs the algorithm's attention to areas of interest. "Explore this customer segment in more detail." "Test the sensitivity of this recommendation to the discount rate." "Show me the cases where you are most confident but might be wrong." The human becomes an explorer, the algorithm a sensing tool.

Trend Three: From Human-in-the-Loop to Loop-in-the-Human

Today's systems are designed around the algorithm. The human is an add-on, called when the algorithm fails.

The future inverts this. In high-stakes domains—surgery, military command, crisis response—the human is the primary decision-maker. The AI is an advisor, providing predictions, risk assessments, and recommendations but never taking action without human authorization. The "loop" is not the algorithm with a human override. It is the human with algorithmic augmentation.

From Synthesis to Leadership

Human-machine synthesis is the operational reality of the AI Factory. It is not a compromise between automation and human judgment. It is a **third way** that achieves what neither could alone: systems that are fast, scalable, consistent, and contextual, resilient, trustworthy.

But synthesis does not happen automatically. It requires design, discipline, and leadership. It requires organizations to move beyond the binary thinking of "man versus machine" and embrace the complexity of partnership. It requires investment in infrastructure for handoffs, training for humans who work alongside algorithms, and metrics that measure team performance, not just component performance.

In Chapter 11, we turn to the leadership that makes this possible. The technical capabilities of the AI Factory, the strategic dynamics of market collisions, the reshaping of work, and the synthesis of human and machine—all depend on leaders who can navigate complexity, make ethical choices, and build organizations that are both powerful and humane.

Operational Element	Role of AI Agent	Role of Human Expert
Information Gathering	**Ingests millions of data points**	**Validates source credibility**
Idea Generation	**Proposes high-volume variations**	**Curation and strategic selection**
Risk Assessment	**Identifies statistical anomalies**	**Evaluates systemic/human impact**
Execution	**Real-time, high-speed delivery**	**Handles exceptions and handoffs**

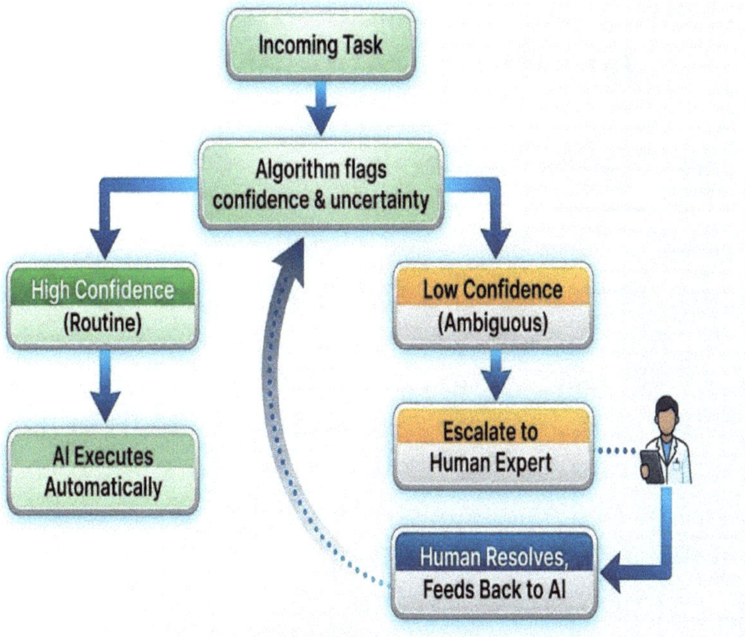

Figure 10: The Handoff Protocol

Chapter 11

The Leadership Mandate: Strategic Upskilling and Organizational Resilience

The New Burden of Leadership

The preceding ten chapters have built a comprehensive picture of the AI-centric firm: the AI Factory with its data pipeline, algorithmic engine, and experimentation platform; the digital backbone of APIs and cloud infrastructure; the virtuous data cycle of network and learning effects; the strategic collisions between digital natives and analog incumbents; the reshaping of work into amplified, rebalanced, enabled, and vulnerable roles; and the human-machine synthesis of orchestrated handoffs.

But none of this happens automatically. Technology does not implement itself. Markets do not restructure themselves. Workforces do not reskill themselves. These transformations require **leadership**—not the incremental leadership of quarterly earnings and annual planning, but the visionary leadership that reimagines what an organization can be and then builds the bridge from here to there.

This chapter outlines the **Leadership Mandate** for the AI age. It is a mandate with four dimensions: strategic upskilling to build workforce capabilities; operating model redesign to align structure with strategy; ecosystem thinking to navigate fluid industry boundaries; and resilience building to withstand the shocks that will inevitably come.

The leaders who answer this mandate will build organizations that thrive. Those who do not will watch their organizations drift into irrelevance—slowly at first, then suddenly.

Strategic Upskilling: Learning as the Core Competency

In the industrial age, skills had a half-life of decades. A machinist trained in the 1970s could practice essentially the same craft in the 1990s. In the AI age, the half-life of technical skills is shrinking toward five years or less. A data scientist who learned Python in 2018 may need to master new frameworks in 2023. A marketer who learned SEO in 2020 must learn prompt engineering in 2024. The pace of change is accelerating, and it will not slow down.

Strategic upskilling is the organizational response to this reality. It is not training. Training is an event: a workshop, a course, a certification. Upskilling is a continuous process. It is embedded in the workday. It is measured, incentivized, and celebrated. It is the mechanism by which the organization ensures that its human capital does not depreciate faster than its physical capital.

The Upskilling Gap

The data on upskilling reveals a stark divide. **"Future-built" companies**—those that have embraced AI as their core operating meta—plan to upskill over 50% of their employees within the next three years. They treat upskilling as a strategic imperative, not an HR program. They budget for it, measure it, and hold leaders accountable for it.

Laggards—firms still operating in the analog mindset—plan to upskill only 20% of their employees. They treat upskilling as an expense to be minimized, a nice-to-have that gets cut when budgets tighten. They assume that they will hire new talent rather than develop existing talent.

The gap is not accidental. It reflects fundamentally different theories of the firm. Laggards see employees as costs to be optimized. Future-built firms see employees as assets to be appreciated. In the AI age, the latter theory wins. The firm that invests in its people will have people who can work with AI. The firm that does not will have people who are displaced by AI.

Building a Learning Culture

Strategic upskilling requires a **learning culture**—an environment where curiosity is rewarded, experimentation is safe, and learning is woven into the fabric of daily work.

Learning in the workflow: The most effective upskilling happens not in classrooms but at desks. When a new AI tool is introduced, employees learn it by using it on real tasks, with real support. Learning is not separate from work; it is work.

Psychological safety: Employees must feel safe to say "I don't know" and to ask for help. In many organizations, admitting ignorance is seen as weakness. In a learning culture, it is seen as the first step toward growth. Leaders model this vulnerability by admitting what they themselves are learning.

Time for learning: The most common barrier to upskilling is time. Employees are measured on output, not on learning. They cannot afford to spend an hour learning a new tool because that hour reduces their productivity metrics. Leaders must change the metrics: allocate a percentage of time (10-20%) for learning, measure learning outcomes, and protect that time against the encroachment of urgent tasks.

Internal knowledge sharing: The organization's best learning resources are its own people. An employee who has mastered a new technique should teach it to others. Internal wikis, lunch-and-learns, and mentorship programs are cheap and effective. The barrier is cultural, not financial.

Identifying Skills Gaps

You cannot upskill effectively if you do not know what skills you need. Strategic upskilling begins with **skills gap analysis**: a systematic assessment of the capabilities the organization has versus the capabilities it will need.

The gap analysis must consider three horizons:

Horizon one (0-12 months): What skills are needed for current operations, but are in short supply? These are immediate hiring or training priorities.

Horizon two (1-3 years): As the AI Factory matures, which roles will be amplified, rebalanced, or enabled? What new skills will those roles require? These are medium-term development priorities.

Horizon three (3-5 years): As the industry evolves and strategic collisions reshape competition, what entirely new capabilities will the organization need? These are long-term, high-uncertainty investments.

Many organizations focus only on horizon one. They fill immediate gaps with contractors or overtime, then wonder why they are always behind. Future-built firms allocate significant attention to horizons two and three, even when horizon one demands are pressing.

The CHRO-CIO-Legal Alliance

Strategic upskilling cannot succeed as a siloed HR initiative. It requires close coordination among three functions that have traditionally operated independently:

The CHRO (Chief Human Resources Officer) owns the talent pipeline: recruitment, development, retention, and career pathing. The CHRO must ensure that upskilling programs exist, that they reach the employees who need them, and that they lead to meaningful career progression.

The CIO (Chief Information Officer) owns the technology infrastructure, including the AI tools that employees must learn. The CIO must ensure that tools are accessible, well-documented, and integrated with learning platforms. The worst upskilling program teaches employees tools they cannot actually use.

Legal and compliance owns the boundaries: data privacy, intellectual property, regulatory compliance. As employees learn to use generative AI tools, legal must provide clear guidance on what is permitted and what is not. Can an employee paste customer data into ChatGPT? (Probably not.) Can they use AI-generated code in production? (Maybe, with review.) Legal must answer these questions before employees start experimenting.

The alliance among these three functions is the **operating system for upskilling**. Without it, programs are fragmented, confused, and ineffective.

Redesigning the Operating Model

Upskilling is necessary but not sufficient. If the organization's structure remains unchanged—the same reporting lines, the same decision rights, the same performance metrics—then upskilled employees will find themselves fighting the system. They will learn to use AI tools, but they will be evaluated on metrics that assume they do not. They will collaborate with algorithms, but their managers will have no training in managing hybrid teams.

Operating model redesign is the companion to upskilling. It is the process of re-architecting how work happens: who decides what, how information flows, how success is measured.

From Hierarchy to Orchestration

The traditional operating model is a hierarchy. Decisions flow down; information flows up. Each layer adds value through aggregation, filtering, and coordination. But as we saw in Chapter 1, the hierarchy imposes a complexity tax. As organizations grow, coordination overhead grows faster than productive output.

The AI-native operating model replaces hierarchy with **orchestration**. The AI Factory handles routine decisions automatically. The digital backbone enables real-time information sharing without managerial intermediaries. The remaining human roles are organized around outcomes, not reporting lines. Teams form around problems, dissolve when problems are solved, and re-form around new problems.

This is not anarchy. It is a different kind of order. The organizing principles are:

- **Decisions go to the lowest competent level** — not the highest available level. The default is delegation, not escalation.
- **Information is shared broadly by default** — not held close as a source of power. The digital backbone makes transparency cheap; the organization must make it cultural.
- **Roles are defined by capabilities, not job titles** — a senior engineer may lead a project; a junior engineer may lead a different project based on their specific expertise.
- **Performance is measured on outcomes, not activities** — not hours worked, not lines of code written, not meetings attended. Did the team achieve its goal?

This operating model is uncomfortable for leaders raised in the hierarchy. They lose the familiar levers of control: approval rights, information asymmetry, positional authority. They gain new levers: context setting, resource allocation, talent development. The transition requires leaders to give up power they once had and learn to wield power they never needed.

The CEO's Role in Redesign

Operating model redesign cannot be delegated. It must be led by the CEO. Only the CEO has the authority to challenge entrenched reporting lines, to eliminate layers of management, to change the metrics by which everyone is evaluated.

The CEO's specific responsibilities include:

Setting the vision: What kind of organization are we building? What will it feel like to work here? What will it be able to do that our current organization cannot? The vision must be concrete enough to guide decisions but aspirational enough to inspire change.

Modeling the new behaviors: If the new operating model values transparency, the CEO must share information broadly—including bad news. If it values psychological safety, the CEO must admit mistakes. If it values continuous learning, the CEO must be visibly learning. Behavior cascades from the top.

Removing structural barriers: The CEO must identify and eliminate the policies, metrics, and reporting lines that conflict with the new model. This is painful work because those barriers exist for a reason—they solved problems in the old model. Removing them creates risk. The CEO must manage that risk while moving forward.

Sustaining the transition: Operating model redesign takes years, not months. The CEO must maintain momentum through inevitable setbacks, leadership changes, and competing priorities. This is the hardest part of the mandate.

Redesigning Governance for AI

The AI Factory introduces new governance challenges that the traditional operating model never anticipated:

Algorithmic decision rights: Who decides what the algorithm optimizes? Who approves a model for deployment? Who is accountable when the algorithm causes harm? These questions must be answered before the algorithm runs, not after.

Model risk management: AI models fail in ways that software does not. They drift. They learn biases. They produce confident wrong answers. The operating model must include processes for model validation, continuous monitoring, and incident response.

Data governance: Who owns the data? Who can access it? For what purposes? These questions are not new, but the scale of data in the AI Factory makes them urgent. Poor data governance leads to privacy violations, compliance failures, and biased models.

The CEO, CHRO, CIO, and legal must together design a governance framework that addresses these challenges without stifling innovation. The framework should be prescriptive enough to prevent disaster and flexible enough to evolve.

Strategic Adaptability and Network Thinking

The AI Factory enables a capability that traditional organizations lack: **strategic adaptability**—the ability to enter adjacent markets, respond to competitive threats, and exploit new opportunities without building new capabilities from scratch.

This adaptability is not automatic. It requires leaders who think in terms of networks, not value chains.

From Value Chains to Ecosystems

The traditional strategic framework is the **value chain**: a linear sequence of activities from raw materials to finished product, with competitive advantage coming from performing those activities better or more cheaply than rivals.

The AI-native framework is the **ecosystem**: a network of interconnected firms, platforms, and customers, with competitive advantage coming from positioning the firm as a hub within that network. The ecosystem is not linear. It is fluid. Value flows in multiple directions. Partners today may be competitors tomorrow.

Leaders who think in value chains ask: "How do we improve our position in this industry?" Leaders who think in ecosystems ask: "What is the role of our platform in the broader network of value creation?"

Strategic Network Analysis

Strategic network analysis is the discipline of mapping the ecosystem—identifying the key nodes, the flows of data and value, the points of leverage and vulnerability.

The analysis answers five questions:

1. **Who are the nodes?** Which firms, platforms, and customer segments are most important in the ecosystem?
2. **What flows between them?** Data? Capital? Customers? Reputation? Each flow has different dynamics.
3. **Where is the power?** Which nodes control access, set standards, or aggregate value? Power may not be where it appears.
4. **Where is the fragility?** Which nodes, if they failed, would disrupt the entire ecosystem?

5.**Where are the opportunities?** Which connections are missing? Which nodes are underserved? Where can the firm insert itself as a new hub?

Strategic network analysis is not a one-time exercise. Ecosystems evolve constantly. New nodes emerge. Old nodes decline. Leaders must refresh their analysis continuously, making it part of the strategic planning rhythm.

Positioning as a Hub

The most valuable position in an ecosystem is the **hub**—the node through which many flows pass. The hub controls access, aggregates value, and sets terms.

How does a firm become a hub? There are three paths:

Owning a critical resource: If the firm controls something that everyone else needs—a unique dataset, a foundational model, a distribution channel—it becomes a hub by necessity. This is the Google/Amazon path.

Solving a coordination problem: If the firm reduces friction in the ecosystem—making it easier for buyers and sellers to find each other, for data to flow, for payments to clear—it becomes a hub by convenience. This is the Stripe/Plaid path.

Building a platform that others extend: If the firm creates a platform that other firms build upon, it becomes a hub by complementarity. This is the Salesforce/ServiceNow path.

Not every firm can become a hub. In every ecosystem, there are many more nodes than hubs. But every firm can understand its position in the network, strengthen its connections, and build resilience against hub power.

Ecosystem Partnerships

Strategic adaptability requires **partnerships**—alliances with other firms that extend the organization's reach without extending its boundaries.

The AI age enables a new kind of partnership: **API-based integration**. Two firms can integrate their capabilities through APIs without equity, without joint ventures, without lengthy contracts. The partnership is expressed in code. It can be turned on and off as strategy evolves.

Leaders must develop a **partnership mindset**: constantly scanning the ecosystem for potential collaborators, evaluating fit, and moving quickly when alignment is found. The partnership mindset is the opposite of the "not invented here" syndrome. It assumes that value comes from orchestration, not ownership.

Organizational Resilience

The AI age will be turbulent. Strategic collisions will disrupt industries. The virtuous data cycle will create winner-take-most dynamics. The half-life of skills will shrink. The only certainty is change.

Organizational resilience is the capacity to absorb shocks, adapt to new conditions, and continue pursuing the mission. Resilience is not robustness—the ability to resist change. It is the ability to change without breaking.

Building Resilience Through Redundancy

In efficiency-obsessed organizations, redundancy is waste. Extra capacity, extra talent, extra systems—these are costs to be eliminated.

In resilient organizations, redundancy is **insurance**. A second cloud provider ensures that the AI Factory keeps running if the primary provider fails. Cross-trained employees ensure that critical functions continue if key individuals leave. Multiple data sources ensure that models can be retrained if one source becomes unavailable.

Leaders must balance efficiency and resilience. Too much efficiency creates brittleness. Too much redundancy creates waste. The right balance depends on the volatility of the environment and the cost of failure.

Building Resilience Through Optionality

Optionality is the ability to take advantage of opportunities as they emerge. It is the opposite of commitment. A firm with optionality has many potential paths and chooses among them as information arrives.

The AI Factory creates optionality by making it cheap to experiment. A new product can be built in weeks, tested on a small audience, and scaled only if it works. This is optionality in product development. A cloud infrastructure that allows the firm to enter new geographies without capital investment is optionality in expansion. A modular architecture that allows the firm to swap out components is optionality in technology.

Leaders must actively preserve optionality. This means resisting the urge to commit too early, to lock in long-term contracts, to build monolithic systems. It means treating strategic decisions as experiments, not final answers.

Building Resilience Through Culture

Ultimately, resilience is cultural. An organization with a learning culture, psychological safety, and a tolerance for failure will absorb shocks that would shatter a brittle, fear-based organization.

Leaders build resilient culture by:

Celebrating learning from failure: When an experiment fails, the question is not "Who is to blame?" but "What did we learn?" The leader who punishes failure trains the organization to hide failure—which ensures that lessons are not learned and mistakes are repeated.

Preparing for the worst: Scenario planning, tabletop exercises, and crisis simulations build muscle memory. When a real crisis arrives, the organization does not freeze. It follows practiced routines.

Communicating honestly: In a crisis, the temptation is to minimize, to reassure, to project confidence. The resilient leader does the opposite: communicates the situation honestly, acknowledges uncertainty, and invites the organization to solve problems together.

The Synthesis of the Mandate

The Leadership Mandate is not a checklist. It is a synthesis of four interconnected responsibilities:

- **Strategic upskilling** ensures that the organization's human capital appreciates, not depreciates.
- **Operating model redesign** ensures that the structure enables, not fights, the capabilities of the AI Factory.
- **Network thinking** ensures that the firm positions itself as a hub within the ecosystem, not a node controlled by others.
- **Resilience building** ensures that the organization survives and thrives through inevitable turbulence.

These responsibilities cannot be delegated. They cannot be outsourced. They cannot be accomplished through a transformation program with a defined end date. They are the ongoing work of leadership in the AI age.

A four-quadrant diagram with a central circle labeled "CEO"

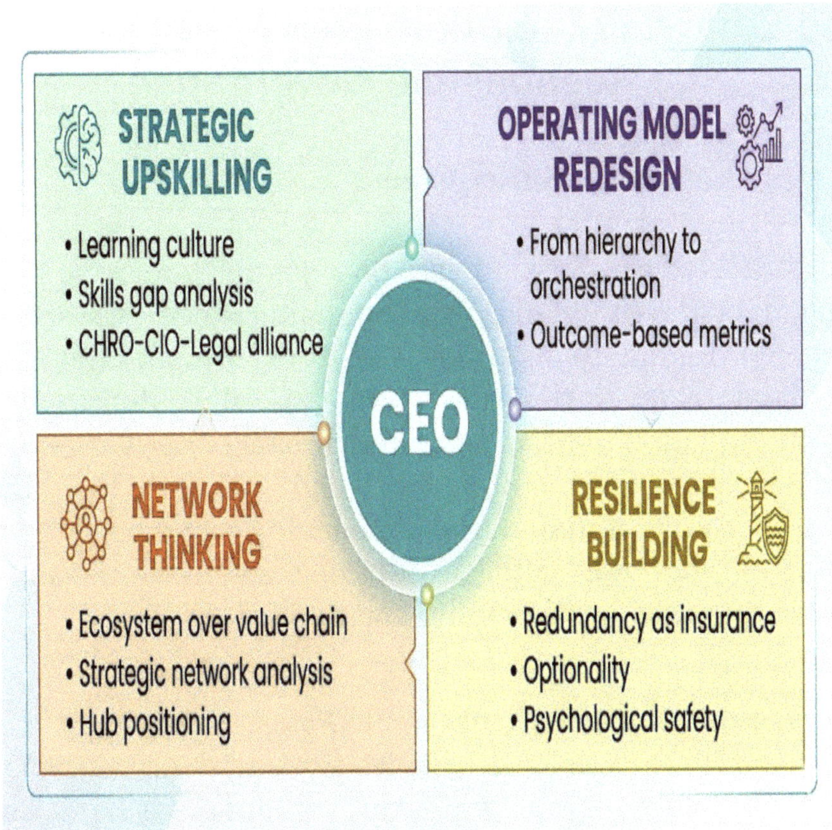

Figure 11.1: The Four Pillars of Leadership

Chapter 12

The Ethical Foundation: Bias Mitigation and Responsible Governance

The Amplification of Consequences

We have traveled a remarkable arc through this book. We began with the inversion of the industrial operating model: the shift from human runtime to algorithmic runtime. We built the AI Factory layer by layer: the data pipeline, the algorithmic engine, the experimentation platform, the digital backbone. We explored the strategic amplification of network and learning effects, the collisions between digital natives and analog incumbents, the reshaping of work, the synthesis of human and machine, and the leadership mandate for upskilling and resilience.

Throughout this journey, we have celebrated the power of the AI Factory. And it is powerful. It enables firms to scale without friction, learn without limit, and adapt without rewiring. It drives productivity gains that were unimaginable a generation ago. It promises to solve problems—in healthcare, climate, education—that have resisted human effort for centuries.

But power without accountability is dangerous. The AI Factory does not just amplify efficiency. It amplifies consequences. A biased hiring algorithm does not reject one candidate; it rejects thousands. A flawed credit model does not deny one loan; it denies millions. An opaque content moderation system does not silence one voice; it shapes the global discourse.

This final chapter confronts the ethical foundation of the AI Factory. We examine the principles of responsible AI, the technical and organizational challenge of bias mitigation, and the broader social responsibilities of firms that have become critical infrastructure. The argument is simple: **trust is the ultimate competitive advantage**. The firms that build AI systems that are fair, transparent, and accountable will attract customers, talent, and regulatory goodwill. The firms that do not will face backlash, regulation, and ultimately obsolescence.

Responsible AI Principles: More Than a Checklist

Responsible AI is not a product feature. It is not a compliance checkbox. It is a design discipline and an organizational culture. It must be embedded from the start, not retrofitted after a crisis.

Three principles define responsible AI in the context of the AI Factory.

Principle One: Proactive, Not Reactive

Most organizations treat AI ethics as a reaction to failure. A biased model is discovered. A scandal erupts. A regulator investigates. The organization responds with a review, a fix, and a promise to do better. The cycle repeats.

Responsible AI is **proactive**. It anticipates failure modes before they occur. It builds guardrails into the system design. It tests for bias, robustness, and transparency before deployment, not after. It assumes that problems will emerge and prepares for them.

Proactive ethics requires a different organizational posture. Instead of asking "Did we comply with regulations?" the organization asks "What could go wrong, and how will we know?" Instead of waiting for external pressure, it builds internal pressure through audits, red teams, and ethical review boards.

Principle Two: Transparent, Not Opaque

The AI Factory produces decisions that affect human lives. Those decisions should be **transparent**—not necessarily in the sense that every weight in the neural network is inspectable (they are not), but in the sense that affected parties can understand why a decision was made and challenge it if it is wrong.

Transparency has multiple dimensions:

Explainability: Can the system provide a human-understandable reason for its decision? "Your loan was denied because your debt-to-income ratio exceeds our threshold" is a meaningful explanation, even if the underlying model is complex.

Auditability: Can independent reviewers examine the system's behavior, test its performance on different subgroups, and verify its compliance with standards? This requires logging decisions, tracking outcomes, and maintaining versioned models.

Redress: When the system makes an error, is there a clear process for appeal? Can a human review the decision and override it if warranted? Redress is the ultimate check on algorithmic power.

Transparency is uncomfortable for organizations that prefer to keep their algorithms secret. But opacity breeds distrust. And in the AI age, distrust is expensive.

Principle Three: Accountable, Not Anonymous

Every decision in the AI Factory should have an accountable human behind it. Not a human who made the decision—the algorithm did that—but a human who is responsible for the system's performance, who can be questioned about its failures, and who is empowered to fix them.

Accountability requires **clear ownership**. For each model, there is a named owner: the person who approves deployment, who monitors performance, who decides when to retrain, who answers when something goes wrong. That owner has authority to make changes and resources to investigate issues.

Accountability also requires **organizational teeth**. The ethics function cannot be advisory; it must have power to block deployment, require remediation, and escalate to the CEO and board. Without enforcement, principles are just words.

Trust as Competitive Advantage

Why should a profit-seeking firm invest in responsible AI? The cynical answer is "to avoid regulation and lawsuits." That answer is true but incomplete. The deeper answer is that **trust is a competitive advantage**.

Consider the alternative. A firm that deploys biased models, that cannot explain its decisions, that has no process for redress—customers will flee when they discover this. Not all customers, perhaps, but enough. The ones who stay will be the ones with fewer choices, the vulnerable populations that the system harms most. Talent will flee too. The best engineers want to work on systems they are proud of, not systems that cause harm.

The firms that earn trust will attract customers who value fairness, employees who value purpose, and regulators who value cooperation. In a world of algorithmic abundance, trust is the scarce resource.

Algorithmic Bias: The Technical Challenge

Algorithmic bias occurs when an AI system produces systematically unfair outcomes for certain groups. Bias can arise at every stage of the AI Factory: in the data, in the algorithm, or in the deployment context.

Bias in the Data

The most common source of bias is the training data. If historical data reflects past discrimination, the model will learn and amplify that discrimination.

Consider a hiring model trained on a company's historical hiring decisions. If the company has historically hired fewer women for technical roles—whether due to explicit bias, pipeline problems, or cultural factors—the model will learn that women are less likely to be successful hires. It will penalize female applicants, not because they are less qualified, but because the data says so.

Similarly, a credit model trained on historical loan data will learn the patterns of past lending. If past lending discriminated against minority neighborhoods—through redlining or other practices—the model will perpetuate that discrimination. It will deny loans to qualified applicants because zip code predicts default in the historical data, even though zip code is a proxy for race, not creditworthiness.

Bias in data is not a bug. It is a feature of learning from human-generated data. Humans are biased. Their decisions reflect that bias. Models trained on those decisions inherit that bias. Removing bias requires intervening on the data or the learning process.

Bias in the Algorithm

Even with unbiased data, algorithms can produce biased outcomes. This happens when the algorithm optimizes for a proxy that correlates with a protected characteristic.

A famous example: a recidivism prediction algorithm used in US courts was found to be biased against Black defendants. The algorithm predicted that Black defendants were at higher risk of reoffending than equally-situated white defendants. The bias did not come from the data—the data included race only indirectly. It came from the algorithm's optimization: it minimized overall prediction error, which led to different false positive rates across groups.

Similarly, a recommendation algorithm that optimizes for engagement may learn that users click more on content that confirms their existing beliefs. It will serve increasingly extreme content, polarizing users and amplifying societal divisions. The bias is not in the data but in the objective function.

Bias in Deployment

Even a perfectly unbiased model can produce biased outcomes if deployed in a biased context. The model interacts with the world, and the world is biased.

Consider a medical diagnostic model that performs equally well across demographic groups in laboratory testing. Deployed in a clinic where Black patients receive less attentive care, the model's recommendations may be followed less consistently, leading to worse outcomes. The bias is not in the model but in the system that uses it.

Or consider a fraud detection model that flags transactions at equal rates across groups. If police disproportionately stop and search minority drivers, the model's flags will lead to more stops of minority drivers—not because the model is biased, but because the deployment context is.

Mitigation Strategies

Bias mitigation is not a one-time fix. It is a continuous discipline woven into the AI Factory's operations.

Diverse data sourcing: The best way to avoid historical bias is to supplement historical data with data that reflects the desired outcomes, not just the past. This might mean oversampling underrepresented groups, generating synthetic data, or using causal models that separate correlation from causation.

Pre-processing debiasing: Transform the training data to remove correlations with protected attributes. This can involve reweighting samples, learning fair representations, or projecting data into a space where protected attributes are not predictable.

In-processing constraints: Modify the learning algorithm to enforce fairness constraints. The algorithm is penalized not just for prediction error but also for disparate impact across groups. This shifts the trade-off: more fairness, less accuracy.

Post-processing calibration: Adjust the model's outputs after training to achieve desired fairness metrics. This might mean setting different decision thresholds for different groups, or calibrating predicted probabilities to be equally calibrated across groups.

Continuous monitoring: Bias can emerge over time as the world changes or as the model drifts. The AI Factory must continuously monitor model performance across subgroups, alerting when disparities exceed thresholds.

None of these strategies is perfect. There are trade-offs between fairness and accuracy, between group fairness and individual fairness, between different definitions of fairness (equality of opportunity vs. demographic parity vs. individual fairness). The technical choices embed value judgments. Those judgments must be made by humans, accountable humans, guided by ethical principles and stakeholder input.

Ethical Governance: The Organizational Challenge

Technical bias mitigation is necessary but not sufficient. The AI Factory also requires **ethical governance**: the organizational structures, processes, and culture that ensure responsible development and deployment.

Governance Structures

Effective ethical governance requires multiple layers:

Ethics review board: A cross-functional body (engineering, legal, product, policy) that reviews high-risk models before deployment. The board asks: What could go wrong? Who might be harmed? What mitigations are in place? The board has authority to block deployment.

Model risk management: A dedicated function that validates models, tests for bias and robustness, and monitors performance in production. This function is independent of the teams that build the models, ensuring objective assessment.

Incident response: A clear process for when things go wrong. Who is notified? Who investigates? Who decides whether to roll back the model? Who communicates with affected users? The process is practiced, not just documented.

Redress mechanism: A channel for users to appeal algorithmic decisions, request human review, and receive explanations. This mechanism is accessible, timely, and effective.

The Leadership Responsibility

Ethical governance cannot be delegated to a "chief ethics officer" or a "responsible AI team." These roles are important, but they are not sufficient. The ultimate responsibility rests with the CEO and the board.

Leadership responsibility includes:

Setting the tone: The CEO communicates that ethics are not a constraint on the business but core to the business. She speaks about fairness, transparency, and accountability in the same breath she speaks about growth and profitability.

Allocating resources: Ethical governance costs money. It requires headcount, tools, and time. The CEO ensures that the ethics function is funded at a level commensurate with the scale and risk of the AI Factory.

Making trade-offs: There are no purely technical solutions to ethical problems. Trade-offs between fairness and accuracy, between different groups, between different values—these are business decisions. The CEO makes them, with input from experts and stakeholders.

Taking accountability: When a model causes harm, the CEO does not blame the data scientists, the product manager, or the algorithm. She takes accountability, makes things right, and ensures it does not happen again.

Regulatory Landscape

The era of unregulated AI is ending. Governments around the world are moving to regulate algorithmic systems.

The European Union's **AI Act** establishes a risk-based framework: unacceptable risk (social scoring, real-time biometric surveillance) is prohibited; high risk (credit scoring, hiring, law enforcement) is subject to strict requirements; limited and minimal risk have lighter touch.

In the United States, there is no comprehensive federal AI regulation yet, but sectoral regulations are emerging. The Equal Employment Opportunity Commission has issued guidance on algorithmic hiring. The Consumer Financial Protection Bureau has stated that adverse action notices apply to algorithmic credit decisions. The Federal Trade Commission has warned that biased algorithms may constitute unfair or deceptive practices.

Other jurisdictions—China, Canada, Brazil, Singapore—are developing their own frameworks. Multinational firms must navigate a patchwork of requirements.

The smartest firms are not waiting for regulation. They are building responsible AI practices now, because they are the right thing to do and because they will be required soon enough.

Beyond Bias: The Broader Social Responsibility

Bias is the most visible ethical challenge of AI, but it is not the only one. The AI Factory raises broader questions of social responsibility.

Mental Health and Addiction

Recommendation algorithms optimized for engagement can become addiction engines. Social media platforms have been criticized for promoting content that maximizes time on site, even when that content is outrage-inducing, anxiety-provoking, or false. The consequences for mental health—especially among adolescents—are severe.

The responsible AI firm asks: What is the objective function? Is it engagement? Or is it well-being? These are not the same. Trade-offs exist. The firm that chooses engagement over well-being may maximize short-term metrics but will face long-term reputational and regulatory costs.

Civil Discourse and Democracy

Platforms that amplify extreme content, reward outrage, and enable coordinated manipulation degrade the quality of civil discourse and threaten democratic institutions. The same algorithms that recommend products can recommend conspiracy theories, hate speech, and disinformation.

The responsible AI firm recognizes that it is not just a technology company but a steward of the public square. This recognition carries obligations: to label synthetic content, to demote disinformation, to provide transparency about algorithmic amplification.

Economic Equality

The AI Factory creates enormous value, but that value is not distributed evenly. The virtuous data cycle concentrates wealth in hub firms and their shareholders. Workers in vulnerable roles face displacement. Communities dependent on traditional industries face decline.

The responsible AI firm asks: How do we share the benefits of AI more broadly? This might mean investing in reskilling, paying fair wages to data labelers, supporting portable benefits for gig workers, or advocating for policies (such as skills-based immigration, education funding, or portable benefits) that spread the gains.

Environmental Impact

Training large AI models consumes massive amounts of energy. A single large language model can emit as much carbon as five cars over their lifetimes. Deploying models at scale—serving billions of predictions—adds to the footprint.

The responsible AI firm considers environmental impact as part of its design process. This might mean choosing more efficient architectures, using renewable energy for training, or optimizing inference to reduce compute per prediction.

The New Social Contract for AI

The AI Factory is not just a business model. It is a new form of social infrastructure. The firms that build and operate these systems wield power that rivals governments. With that power comes responsibility.

The **new social contract** for AI has three pillars:

Rights for individuals: People have the right to know when they are interacting with an AI system, to receive explanations of algorithmic decisions that affect them, to appeal those decisions to a human, and to be free from algorithmic discrimination.

Obligations for firms: Firms that deploy AI systems have the obligation to test for bias and harm, to monitor continuously, to respond to incidents transparently, and to submit to independent audit.

Accountability for leaders: Executives and boards are accountable for the consequences of their AI systems. They cannot hide behind technical complexity or diffuse responsibility. They own the outcomes.

This social contract is not yet written into law. But it is emerging in court rulings, regulatory guidance, and public expectations. The firms that embrace it will thrive. The firms that resist it will be forced to comply anyway—after the scandals, after the lawsuits, after the reputational damage.

The Competitive Advantage of Trust

We return to the core argument: **trust is the ultimate competitive advantage**.

In the industrial age, trust was nice to have. Customers bought from whoever offered the best price and quality. Trust was a tiebreaker, not a primary driver.

In the AI age, trust is essential. The AI Factory knows more about customers than they know about themselves. It makes decisions that affect their lives in ways they cannot fully understand. Customers will not engage with systems they do not trust. They will not share data with firms they believe will misuse it. They will not accept decisions from algorithms they believe are biased.

The firms that earn trust will capture the virtuous data cycle. Customers will share data because they trust the firm to use it responsibly. That data will improve the models, which will attract more customers, which will generate more data. Trust is not a constraint on the cycle. It is the fuel.

The firms that lose trust will find the cycle working against them. Customers will withhold data. Regulators will impose restrictions. Talent will leave. The cycle will spin in reverse.

The New Meta, Revisited

In Chapter 1, we defined the AI age as a new operating meta: the shift from human runtime to algorithmic runtime. We argued that the first dramatic implications of AI are not the simulation of human consciousness but the transformation of organizational nature.

Now, at the end of this book, we add a corollary. The transformation of organizational nature carries with it a transformation of organizational responsibility. The firm that runs on algorithms, that scales without friction, that learns without limit—that firm is not just a competitor in a market. It is a shaper of society.

The leaders of these firms did not ask for this responsibility. But they cannot escape it. The power of the AI Factory is too great, its consequences too profound, for its operators to claim neutrality. Every choice about what to optimize, what data to collect, what handoffs to design, what thresholds to set—these are ethical choices. They reflect values. They have consequences.

The new meta of AI competition requires a new meta of leadership. Technical excellence is not enough. Strategic brilliance is not enough. The leaders who will define the next century are those who combine technical mastery with ethical clarity, who build organizations that are both powerful and principled, who understand that trust is not a constraint on growth but the foundation of it.

Coda: The Unfinished Revolution

This book is a map, not a destination. The AI Factory is still being built. The virtuous data cycle is still spinning up. The strategic collisions are still unfolding. The workforce is still being reshaped. The ethical foundation is still being laid.

We are in the early innings of a revolution that will unfold over decades. The firms that win will not be those with the best algorithms today. They will be those that learn fastest, that adapt most nimbly, that build the most trusted relationships with customers, employees, and society.

The industrial age took a century to fully transform how we work, live, and relate to one another. The AI age will move faster. Much faster. The leaders who read this book are not preparing for a future that is distant. They are building it now.

The factory does not rest. Neither can they.

Figure 12: The Responsible AI Stack

Below the pyramid, a table of mitigation strategies:

Bias Source	**Mitigation**
Biased training data	Diverse data sourcing, pre-processing debiasing
Algorithmic optimization	In-processing fairness constraints
Deployment context	Continuous monitoring, human oversight

Caption: Responsible AI is not a checklist. It is a stack of capabilities, each building on the one below.

Chapter 13

Leadership in the Age of AI

The Unprecedented Burden

Throughout this book, we have described the AI Factory, the virtuous data cycle, the strategic collisions, the reshaping of work, and the ethical foundation. We have explained what organizations must become to thrive in the age of AI. But we have not yet fully addressed the person at the top—the leader who must make it happen.

Leadership in the age of AI is different from leadership in the industrial age. It is not just faster or more demanding. It is qualitatively different. The old leadership playbook—command and control, annual planning, hierarchical decision-making—was designed for a world of scarce information and slow change. That world is gone. The new world demands new leadership capabilities.

This chapter distills the leadership implications of the entire book into a practical framework. We identify new executive responsibilities, examine the integration of ethical governance into leadership practice, explore the challenge of organizational redesign from the top, and describe how leaders build a culture of experimentation that sustains the AI Factory over time.

New Executive Responsibilities

The CEO of an AI-centric firm has responsibilities that did not exist a decade ago. Some of these are technical; most are organizational and cultural.

Responsibility One: Architecting the AI Factory

The CEO does not need to write code or train models. But the CEO must understand the architecture of the AI Factory well enough to make strategic trade-offs. How much to invest in data infrastructure versus algorithmic development? When to build versus buy? How to balance automation with human oversight?

These are not technical questions. They are strategic questions with technical implications. The CEO who delegates them entirely to the CTO or CIO is abdicating responsibility. The CEO must be fluent enough in the language of data and algorithms to ask the right questions, evaluate competing proposals, and hold technical leaders accountable.

This does not mean every CEO needs a computer science degree. It does mean every CEO needs sufficient literacy to understand what AI can and cannot do, where the risks are, and how to measure progress.

Responsibility Two: Owning the Virtuous Data Cycle

In Chapter 7, we described the virtuous data cycle: more users generate more data, better models attract more users. This cycle is the engine of competitive advantage in the AI age. But it does not run itself.

The CEO must own the cycle. This means asking: Are we collecting the right data? Are we using it to improve our products? Are we closing the feedback loop from decisions to outcomes? Are our data practices building trust or eroding it? The

CEO who does not ask these questions will find that competitors with better cycles have captured the market.

Owning the cycle also means making uncomfortable trade-offs. Data collection that improves models may also raise privacy concerns. Aggressive customer acquisition may short-term boost the cycle but long-term damage trust. The CEO must navigate these trade-offs with a clear eye on both immediate metrics and long-term position.

Responsibility Three: Leading the Workforce

Transformation

In Chapter 9, we described the reshaping of work into amplified, rebalanced, enabled, and vulnerable categories. This transformation does not happen automatically. It requires active leadership.

The CEO must champion upskilling—not as an HR program but as a strategic imperative. This means allocating budget, protecting time for learning, and holding managers accountable for developing their people. It means communicating honestly about which roles are changing and why. It means treating displaced workers with dignity, investing in reskilling even when severance would be cheaper.

The CEO who ignores workforce transformation will find that the organization cannot execute its AI strategy. The technology may be ready, but the people will not be. And people—not algorithms—are ultimately what make organizations work.

Responsibility Four: Governing Algorithmic Risk

In Chapter 12, we described the ethical foundations of responsible AI. The CEO must own the governance of algorithmic risk. This means ensuring that the organization has the structures—review boards, risk management functions, incident response processes—to catch problems before they cause harm. It means setting the tone that ethics are not a constraint but a core value. It means taking accountability when things go wrong.

The CEO who delegates algorithmic risk to the legal department or the compliance function is making a dangerous mistake. Lawyers and compliance officers are trained to manage regulatory risk, not ethical risk. The two are related but not identical. Ethical risk—loss of trust, damage to brand, harm to stakeholders—is ultimately the CEO's responsibility.

Responsibility Five: Communicating the AI Strategy

The AI Factory is complex. Most employees, customers, and investors will not understand how it works. The CEO must translate complexity into clarity.

This means explaining, in plain language, what the organization is doing with AI and why. It means being honest about limitations and risks. It means articulating a vision that inspires without overselling. It means answering hard questions from the board, the press, and the public.

The CEO who cannot communicate the AI strategy will struggle to align the organization, attract talent, or maintain trust.

Communication is not a soft skill. It is an executive responsibility as critical as any other.

Ethical Governance as Leadership Practice

Ethical governance is not a compliance function. It is a leadership practice. The CEO who treats ethics as something to be managed by a separate committee has already failed.

Embedding Ethics in Strategy

The most important ethical decisions are not about preventing bad outcomes. They are about choosing which outcomes to pursue. What objective function should the algorithm optimize? Engagement or well-being? Efficiency or fairness? Short-term revenue or long-term trust?

These are strategic choices, not technical ones. They reflect the values of the organization. The CEO must make them explicitly, not default to whatever is easiest to measure. And the CEO must be prepared to defend them to stakeholders who may disagree.

Creating Psychological Safety for Ethical Concerns

In many organizations, employees who raise ethical concerns are punished—not explicitly, but through exclusion, marginalization, and career stagnation. The message is clear: do not rock the boat.

The CEO must reverse this dynamic. This means creating psychological safety: an environment where employees feel safe speaking up about potential harms, biases, or unintended consequences. It means thanking employees who raise concerns, not punishing them. It means investigating every credible report and taking action when problems are found.

Psychological safety is not soft. It is the prerequisite for ethical governance. Without it, the organization is flying blind.

Modeling Ethical Behavior

The CEO's behavior sets the norm for the entire organization. If the CEO cuts ethical corners, everyone will. If the CEO treats transparency as optional, everyone will. If the CEO dismisses concerns as "just the cost of doing business," everyone will.

The CEO who wants an ethical organization must model ethical behavior. This means being transparent about decisions, admitting mistakes, and holding oneself accountable. It means making trade-offs that favor long-term trust over short-term gain, even when no one is watching. It means living the values the organization professes.

Organizational Redesign from the Top

The organizational structures designed for the industrial age are not suitable for the AI age. Hierarchy, silos, and rigid reporting lines impede the data flows and rapid adaptation that the AI Factory requires. But redesigning an organization is perilous. Done poorly, it creates chaos, destroys morale, and undermines performance.

The CEO must lead redesign with a clear framework and a steady hand.

Principles of AI-Centric Organizational Design

Based on the preceding chapters, we can derive several principles for AI-centric organizational design:

Data flows instead of reporting lines: In a traditional hierarchy, information moves up and decisions move down. In an AI-centric organization, data flows horizontally through shared pipelines and feature stores. Reporting lines become less important than data access.

Teams organized around outcomes, not functions: Functional silos (marketing, sales, product, engineering) optimize locally but suboptimally globally. AI-centric organizations organize cross-functional teams around customer outcomes, giving them the data, models, and authority to achieve those outcomes.

Decision rights pushed to the edge: The AI Factory automates routine decisions. The remaining human decisions should be made at the lowest competent level, not escalated up the hierarchy. This requires trust, transparency, and clear decision criteria.

Modularity over integration: Tightly coupled systems are brittle. Loosely coupled services with well-defined APIs are resilient. The same principle applies to organizational units: they should be modular, with clear interfaces and minimal dependencies.

Continuous learning as a core process: The AI Factory learns continuously from data. The organization should learn continuously from experiments. This requires processes for capturing lessons, sharing knowledge, and updating practices.

The Redesign Process

Organizational redesign cannot be done in a weekend retreat. It is a multi-year journey. The CEO must manage it as such.

Phase One: Diagnosis. Before redesigning, understand the current state. Where are the bottlenecks? Where does information flow poorly? Where do silos impede collaboration? Where does the hierarchy add delay without adding value? This diagnosis should be data-driven, not anecdotal.

Phase Two: Pilot. Do not redesign the entire organization at once. Select one division, one product line, or one geography as a pilot. Redesign that unit according to AI-centric principles. Measure the results. Learn what works and what does not.

Phase Three: Scale. Once the pilot has demonstrated success, scale the new model to other units. This is not a copy-paste. Each unit will have unique characteristics. Adapt the principles to local context, but maintain the core philosophy.

Phase Four: Iterate. The first redesign will not be the last. As the AI Factory evolves, the organization must evolve with it. Build a continuous redesign capability: regular reviews, learning loops, and the authority to make changes without waiting for a multi-year transformation program.

The Role of the CEO in Redesign

The CEO cannot delegate redesign. But the CEO also cannot micromanage it. The right role is:

Vision setter: Articulating the destination—what the organization will look like and how it will operate—without prescribing every detail of the path.

Barrier remover: Identifying and eliminating the structural, cultural, and political barriers that prevent redesign from succeeding. This often means overruling senior leaders who benefit from the old structures.

Resource allocator: Ensuring that redesign efforts have the budget, talent, and attention they need. This means taking resources from business-as-usual activities and redirecting them to transformation.

Chief cheerleader: Celebrating wins, learning from failures, and maintaining momentum through the inevitable setbacks. Redesign is exhausting. The CEO's energy and optimism are renewable resources that the organization depends on.

Building a Culture of Experimentation

The AI Factory depends on continuous experimentation (Chapter 5). But experimentation is not just a technical capability. It is a cultural one. The CEO must build a culture where experimentation is the norm, not the exception.

The Components of an Experimentation Culture

Hypothesis-driven decision-making: Instead of arguing about opinions, the organization asks: "What would we need to see to change our mind?" and "How can we test that?" Decisions are framed as hypotheses, not conclusions.

Tolerance for failure: Experiments fail. That is the point. The organization learns from failure without punishing it. The only unacceptable failure is the experiment that was never run because everyone was afraid to be wrong.

Rapid feedback loops: The organization shortens cycle times between "idea" and "measurement." Weekly experiments instead of quarterly, daily instead of weekly, hourly instead of daily. Speed matters because learning compounds.

Data accessibility: Everyone who needs data to run experiments can access it—subject to privacy and security constraints, but not to bureaucratic gatekeeping. Data is a shared resource, not a proprietary asset.

Statistical literacy: Everyone who interprets experimental results understands p-values, confidence intervals, and the difference between correlation and causation. This is not a specialized skill for data scientists; it is a core competency for all decision-makers.

The CEO's Role in Building Experimentation Culture

The CEO's most powerful tool for building culture is **attention**. What the CEO pays attention to signals what matters.

When the CEO asks "What did we learn this week?" not "Did we hit our numbers?"—that signals that learning matters. When the CEO celebrates a well-run experiment that produced a null result—that signals that failure is acceptable. When the CEO asks for the confidence interval, not just the point estimate—that signals that statistical rigor matters.

The CEO also models the culture by running experiments on their own decisions. Test two different formats for the weekly all-hands. A/B test the subject lines of internal communications. Run a controlled trial of a new meeting structure. When the CEO experiments, everyone gets permission to experiment.

Overcoming Resistance to Experimentation

Many organizations resist experimentation. The reasons are cultural, not technical: fear of failure, fear of losing control, fear of looking foolish. The CEO must address these fears directly.

Addressing fear of failure: Frame failure as learning. Celebrate the lessons from failed experiments publicly. Ensure that careers are not damaged by well-designed experiments that produced null results.

Addressing fear of losing control: Show that experimentation does not undermine authority; it informs it. The leader still makes the final call, but with better information. Experimentation is a tool for better decisions, not a replacement for judgment.

Addressing fear of looking foolish: Create psychological safety. The CEO admits their own mistakes, thanks people who point out errors, and models intellectual humility. Looking foolish is the price of learning.

The Leader as Learner

Underlying all of these responsibilities is a single meta-capability: **learning**. The AI age changes too fast for any leader to have all the answers. The leader who cannot learn—who is wedded to past success, who cannot admit gaps in knowledge, who cannot adapt—will fail.

The leader as learner has four habits:

Curiosity: Asking questions, not just giving answers. Seeking out perspectives that challenge assumptions. Reading widely outside one's industry. Staying humble about what one does not know.

Reflection: Making time to think, not just react. Reviewing decisions to understand what worked and what did not. Updating mental models based on new evidence.

Feedback-seeking: Actively asking for criticism, not just praise. Creating mechanisms for anonymous feedback. Thanking people who point out blind spots.

Reteaching: Explaining what one has learned to others. Teaching crystallizes understanding and spreads knowledge throughout the organization.

The leader who learns will keep pace with the AI age. The leader who does not will be left behind—and will take their organization with them.

The Personal Journey

Leading in the age of AI is not just a professional challenge. It is a personal one. The leader must confront their own relationship with technology, with uncertainty, and with power.

Confronting technical anxiety: Many leaders feel anxious about their lack of technical depth. They fear being exposed as ignorant. The solution is not to pretend expertise but to embrace curiosity. Ask naive questions. Admit what you do not know. Learn alongside your team.

Confronting uncertainty: The AI age is unpredictable. No one knows exactly how capabilities will evolve, which business models will win, or how regulation will shape the landscape. The leader who needs certainty will be paralyzed. The leader who can act with incomplete information—who can make bets, learn, and pivot—will thrive.

Confronting power: The AI age concentrates power. Hub firms control critical infrastructure. Algorithms make decisions that affect millions of lives. Leaders who are uncomfortable with power—who deny it, deflect it, or abuse it—will fail. The leader must accept power, wield it responsibly, and remain accountable for its use.

This is heavy work. It requires self-awareness, humility, and courage. Not every leader is suited for it. But for those who are, the opportunity is extraordinary: to build organizations that are more productive, more creative, more fair, and more human than anything that came before.

From Leadership to Legacy

This book has described a transformation. The AI Factory. The virtuous data cycle. Strategic collisions. The reshaping of work. The ethical foundation. These are the building blocks of the organization of the future.

But organizations do not transform themselves. Leaders transform them. Leaders set the vision, allocate the resources, remove the barriers, and model the behaviors. Leaders take the risk. Leaders accept the accountability.

The leaders who succeed in the AI age will leave a legacy. They will have built organizations that used AI not just to extract value but to create it—for customers, for employees, for shareholders, for society. They will have navigated the ethical minefields without losing their way. They will have transformed work without dehumanizing workers. They will have competed fiercely without compromising their values.

That is the leadership mandate. It is not easy. It is not for everyone. But it is the work of our time.

The factory does not rest. Neither can its leaders.

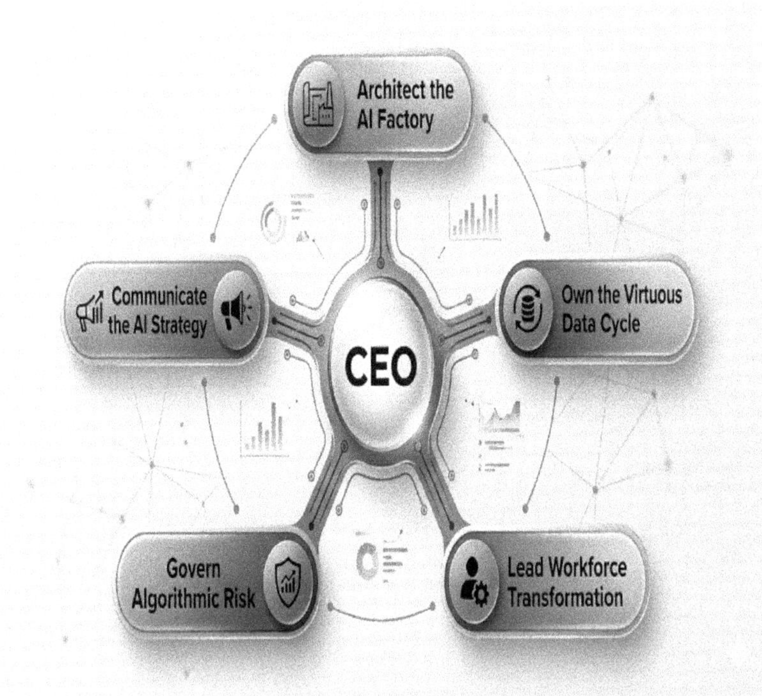

Figure 13: The Five CEO Responsibilities

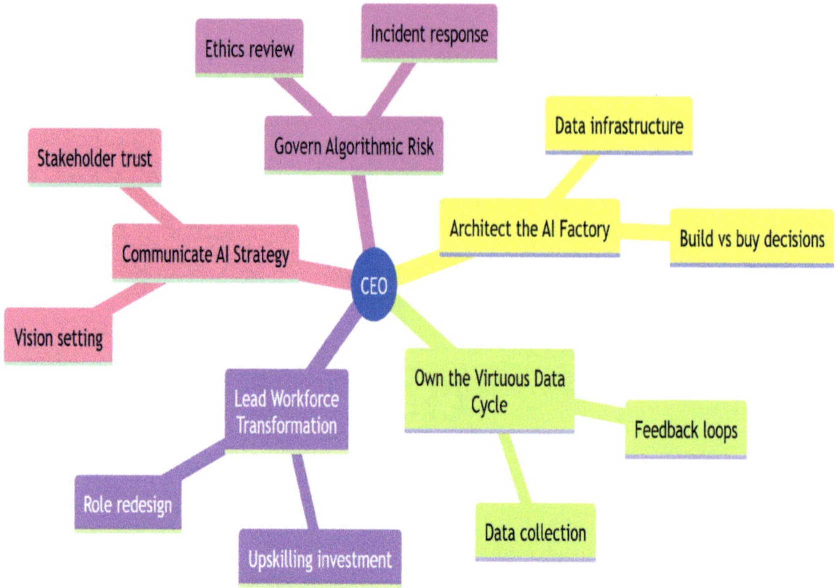
CEO
Govern Algorithmic Risk
Ethics review
Incident response
Architect the AI Factory
Data infrastructure
Build vs buy decisions
Own the Virtuous Data Cycle
Feedback loops
Data collection
Lead Workforce Transformation
Role redesign
Upskilling investment
Communicate AI Strategy
Stakeholder trust
Vision setting

Chapter 14: Accelerating Learning

The Learning Race

In the industrial age, competitive advantage came from scale: producing more units at lower cost per unit. In the AI age, competitive advantage comes from learning: processing more transactions at higher intelligence per transaction. The firm that learns fastest wins.

But what does it mean for an organization to learn? In traditional organizations, learning is episodic: a quarterly review, a post-mortem, a training session. Learning happens between the work, not during it. The pace is slow, the lessons are diffuse, and the impact is uncertain.

In the AI Factory, learning is continuous. Every transaction generates a signal. Every signal updates a model. Every updated model improves the next transaction. The cycle is measured in milliseconds, not months. The pace is relentless, the lessons are precise, and the impact is compounding.

This chapter explores the mechanisms that accelerate learning in the AI-centric firm: continuous experimentation, A/B testing at scale, and automated model retraining. These are not separate activities. They are integrated components of a single learning system—a system that turns the AI Factory into a perpetual motion machine of improvement.

The Anatomy of Learning

Before diving into mechanisms, we must understand what learning means in the context of the AI Factory. There are three distinct types of learning, each with its own pace and purpose.

Type One: Model Learning

Model learning is the most granular form of learning. Every time the AI Factory makes a prediction and observes the outcome, it has an opportunity to update its model. A fraud detection model predicts that a transaction is legitimate. The transaction later proves to be fraudulent. That signal—the model was wrong—can be used to update the model's parameters, making it less likely to make the same mistake in the future.

Model learning is automatic. It does not require human intervention. It happens continuously, in real time or in batch, depending on the architecture. The rate of model learning is limited only by the volume of transactions and the computational budget for retraining.

Type Two: Experimental Learning

Experimental learning occurs when the organization deliberately tests a change to understand its causal effect. Unlike model learning, which improves predictions within the existing system, experimental learning improves the system itself. A new feature, a different algorithm, an alternative workflow—these are tested through controlled experiments to determine whether they outperform the status quo.

Experimental learning requires human direction. Someone must formulate the hypothesis, design the experiment, and decide whether to roll out the change. But the execution can be automated: the experimentation platform handles randomization, data collection, and statistical analysis.

Type Three: Organizational Learning

Organizational learning is the slowest but most profound form of learning. It occurs when the organization changes its processes, structures, or strategies based on accumulated experience. A team discovers that a particular workflow is inefficient and redesigns it. A leader realizes that a certain metric is misleading and replaces it. The organization internalizes lessons from multiple experiments and model updates, then changes how it operates.

Organizational learning requires reflection. It is not automatic. It must be supported by rituals—retrospectives, post-mortems, knowledge-sharing forums—that translate raw data into shared understanding.

The AI-centric firm excels at all three types of learning. Model learning happens in milliseconds. Experimental learning happens in days or weeks. Organizational learning happens in months or quarters. Each type reinforces the others, creating a virtuous cycle of accelerating improvement.

Continuous Experimentation: The Engine of Discovery

In traditional organizations, experimentation is an event. A team runs a test, analyzes the results, and presents findings. Months may pass between experiments. The organization learns slowly because it tests rarely.

In the AI Factory, experimentation is **continuous**. The organization runs hundreds or thousands of experiments simultaneously, each testing a different hypothesis, each generating data that feeds into the next. The experimentation platform is always active. There is no "testing phase" followed by a "production phase." The system is always in both modes.

The Continuous Experimentation Loop

Continuous experimentation follows a closed loop:

1. **Hypothesize**: A product manager, data scientist, or engineer proposes a change. "If we change the recommendation algorithm from collaborative filtering to a neural network, click-through rate will increase by 5%."
2. **Configure**: The team configures an experiment in the experimentation platform: the treatment (the new algorithm), the control (the existing algorithm), the target population (which users), the success metrics (click-through rate, but also watch time, retention, and revenue), and the duration (until statistical power is achieved).
3. **Execute**: The platform randomly assigns users to treatment or control, serves the appropriate experience, and logs all outcomes. No human intervention is required during this phase.
4. **Analyze**: When the experiment reaches its planned duration, the platform automatically analyzes the results. It computes effect sizes, confidence intervals, and statistical significance. It flags whether the treatment outperformed the control.
5. **Decide**: A human reviews the analysis. If the treatment is superior, it is rolled out to all users. If it is inferior, it is discarded. If the results are inconclusive, the team decides whether to extend the experiment or abandon the hypothesis.

6.**Learn**: Regardless of the outcome, the results are recorded in a shared knowledge base. Future experimenters can query past results, avoiding redundant tests and building on prior learning.

The loop repeats continuously. At any given moment, dozens or hundreds of experiments are in flight, at different stages of the loop. The organization learns in parallel, not in series.

The Infrastructure for Continuous Experimentation

Continuous experimentation requires infrastructure that traditional organizations lack:

Feature flags: The ability to turn features on and off without deploying new code. Feature flags enable experiments to be configured dynamically, without engineering lead time.

Randomization engine: A reliable service that assigns users to treatment or control in a way that is deterministic (the same user always gets the same assignment for a given experiment) but unpredictable (no systematic bias).

Metrics pipeline: A real-time or near-real-time system that computes success metrics from raw logs. Experimenters need results quickly, not in next quarter's reporting cycle.

Statistical engine: Automated statistical testing that correctly handles multiple comparisons, peeking, and early stopping. The platform must protect experimenters from common statistical pitfalls.

Knowledge base: A searchable repository of past experiments, including hypotheses, designs, results, and decisions. The knowledge base prevents teams from running the same experiment twice and helps them build on prior work.

The Cultural Shift

The technical infrastructure is necessary but not sufficient. Continuous experimentation also requires a cultural shift.

From opinions to hypotheses: In traditional organizations, decisions are made by the loudest voice or the highest rank. In an experimentation culture, decisions are made by evidence. Anyone can propose a hypothesis. The experiment decides.

From fear of failure to celebration of learning: An experiment that shows no effect—or a negative effect—is not a failure. It is a successful test of a hypothesis. The organization learns not to pursue that change. The only true failure is the hypothesis that was never tested because everyone was afraid to be wrong.

From slow consensus to fast action: Traditional decision-making requires alignment across multiple stakeholders. Experimentation short-circuits this process. Run the test. Get the answer. Act on it. No meeting required.

The CEO must model this culture by running experiments on their own decisions, celebrating null results, and asking "What did we learn?" not "Did we win?"

A/B Testing at Scale

A/B testing is the most common form of continuous experimentation. The name comes from the two variants: A (control) and B (treatment). But modern A/B testing is far more sophisticated than a simple two-way comparison.

Beyond Simple A/B Tests

Multivariate tests simultaneously test multiple variations. Instead of comparing one new algorithm to the old algorithm, a multivariate test might compare three different algorithms, two different user interface layouts, and four different pricing strategies—all in the same experiment. The sample size must be larger to detect effects, but the learning per customer is higher.

Bandit experiments dynamically allocate more users to better-performing variants during the experiment, rather than waiting until the end to declare a winner. This is more efficient (fewer users are exposed to inferior treatments) and more ethical (the platform learns faster and serves better experiences sooner). The trade-off is statistical complexity: bandit experiments require sequential analysis rather than fixed-horizon tests.

Interleaving experiments compare two ranking algorithms by interleaving their results in a single list presented to the user. If algorithm A's results are clicked more often than algorithm B's results, even though the user did not know which came from which, A is superior. Interleaving is statistically efficient (it requires fewer users than traditional A/B tests) but only works for ranking problems.

Network A/B tests account for interference between users. In a traditional A/B test, we assume that the treatment assigned to one user does not affect the outcomes of other users. This assumption is violated in social networks, marketplaces, and any setting where users interact. Network A/B tests use cluster randomization (assigning whole groups to treatment or control) or ego network designs to isolate causal effects.

The Scale of Modern A/B Testing

The scale of A/B testing at leading digital firms is staggering.

Amazon runs thousands of experiments simultaneously, affecting millions of customers. Everything from the placement of the buy button to the algorithm powering product recommendations is continuously tested. A change that improves conversion by 0.1% is worth millions of dollars annually and is rolled out immediately.

Netflix runs hundreds of experiments at any given time, testing not just product features but also the artwork displayed for each title. A single movie thumbnail might be tested across dozens of variants, with different images shown to different audience segments. The goal is not to find the best thumbnail for everyone but to learn which images drive engagement for which types of content for which types of viewers.

Microsoft runs A/B tests on almost every change to its Office, Windows, and Bing products. The company has built an internal experimentation platform called "ExP" that handles billions of user assignments per day. The platform automatically analyzes results, applies statistical corrections for multiple comparisons, and recommends roll-out decisions.

Google runs experiments on everything from search ranking algorithms to ad auction mechanics to Gmail interface changes. The company estimates that it runs tens of thousands of experiments per year, with many running concurrently. The cumulative effect of these experiments—each contributing a tiny improvement—is massive.

The Organizational Requirements for A/B Testing at Scale

Achieving this scale requires more than technology. It requires organizational discipline.

Shared experimentation platform: A single platform used by all teams, not separate tools for each department. A shared platform enables consistent statistical methods, shared knowledge, and efficient use of traffic.

Experimentation governance: Clear rules about when experiments are required, how long they must run, and what thresholds must be met for roll-out. Governance prevents teams from cherry-picking results or stopping experiments early when they see a "win."

Traffic management: Experiments compete for user traffic. A user cannot be in fifty experiments at once without statistical contamination. The platform must manage traffic allocation, ensuring that experiments have sufficient sample size without interfering with each other.

Statistical expertise: Even with automated platforms, organizations need statisticians who understand the nuances of sequential testing, multiple comparisons, and network interference. These experts audit experiments, troubleshoot anomalies, and train the broader organization.

Model Retraining: Keeping Intelligence Fresh

Experimentation improves the system. Model retraining improves the predictions. Both are essential. But model retraining has its own dynamics and challenges.

Why Models Need Retraining

Models degrade over time. The world changes. Customer preferences shift. Competitors change their strategies. The data distribution that the model was trained on drifts away from the current reality.

This phenomenon is called **model drift** or **concept drift**. It has three causes:

Data drift: The distribution of input features changes. Credit applicants today have different characteristics than credit applicants five years ago. Sensor readings change as equipment ages. The model's inputs no longer look like what it was trained on.

Label drift: The relationship between inputs and outputs changes. A fraud pattern that was predictive last year may be irrelevant today because fraudsters have adapted. A recommendation that led to purchases last quarter may lead to clicks but not purchases this quarter because user behavior has changed.

Environmental change: The underlying environment shifts. A pandemic changes consumer behavior. A new regulation changes underwriting standards. A competitor's new product changes what customers expect. The model's assumptions are violated.

Retraining Strategies

Organizations choose among three retraining strategies, each with different trade-offs.

Batch retraining: The model is retrained periodically—daily, weekly, or monthly—on all accumulated data since the last retraining. Batch retraining is simple to implement and ensures that the model incorporates all available data. The trade-off is latency: the model may be stale between retraining cycles.

Continuous retraining: The model is updated incrementally with each new batch of data. Instead of retraining from scratch, the model's parameters are adjusted based on new examples. Continuous retraining keeps the model fresh but requires more sophisticated infrastructure to avoid overfitting to recent data.

Trigger-based retraining: The model is retrained when performance degrades below a threshold. Monitoring systems track prediction accuracy, calibration, and other metrics. When performance falls below the threshold, a retraining job is triggered. Trigger-based retraining is efficient (retraining only when needed) but requires robust monitoring.

The Retraining Pipeline

Retraining is not a one-click operation. It is a pipeline with multiple stages:

1. **Data extraction**: Pull new labeled data from the data warehouse or feature store. The data must include both features (inputs) and labels (outcomes) since the last retraining.
2. **Data validation**: Check that the new data is consistent with the old data. Detect data drift, missing values, or schema changes that could break the model.
3. **Training**: Run the training algorithm on the combined historical data (old + new) or on a rolling window. This is computationally expensive, especially for large models.
4. **Validation**: Evaluate the retrained model on holdout data. Compare its performance to the current production model. If the retrained model is not better, do not deploy it.
5. **Deployment**: Push the retrained model to production, replacing the current model. This may involve a canary deployment (route a small percentage of traffic to the new model) or a blue-green deployment (switch traffic atomically).
6. **Monitoring**: Track the performance of the retrained model in production. Watch for unexpected degradation or bias. Be prepared to roll back if problems emerge.

Automated vs. Human-in-the-Loop Retraining

The tension in retraining is the same as in other AI processes: automation versus human oversight.

Fully automated retraining retrains and deploys without human intervention. This is appropriate for low-stakes models where errors are cheap and the environment changes quickly. A recommendation model that occasionally recommends a bad product is annoying but not catastrophic.

Human-in-the-loop retraining requires human approval before deployment. A human reviews the validation results, checks for bias, and signs off on the update. This is appropriate for high-stakes models where errors are costly. A credit scoring model that becomes systematically biased could cause serious harm.

Most organizations use a hybrid: automated retraining for low-stakes models, human approval for high-stakes models, and automated monitoring that alerts humans when something unusual occurs.

Integrating Experimentation and Retraining

Experimentation and retraining are often treated as separate activities. They are not. They are two sides of the same learning coin.

Experimentation changes the system. Retraining updates the model. But the two interact. An experiment that changes the user interface will change the data distribution that the model sees. A model that is retrained on post-experiment data will learn the new patterns. The learning accelerates.

The integrated learning system works as follows:

1. **Baseline**: The production model serves predictions. The system runs in steady state.
2. **Experimentation**: An experiment tests a change to the system —a new feature, a different workflow, an alternative algorithm. The experiment randomly assigns users to treatment or control.
3. **Data collection**: Both treatment and control groups generate data. The data includes features, predictions, outcomes, and experiment assignment.

4.**Causal analysis**: The experiment analyzes the data to estimate the causal effect of the change. If the change is beneficial, it is rolled out to all users.
5.**Model retraining**: After the change is rolled out, the model is retrained on the new data. The retrained model incorporates the new patterns. The system is now better than before the experiment.
6.**Repeat**: The cycle begins again. Each experiment makes the system better. Each retraining makes the model smarter. Learning accelerates.

This integration is the engine of competitive advantage. The firm that experiments continuously and retrains automatically will out-learn any firm that treats these as occasional activities.

The Metrics of Learning

How do you know if your organization is learning fast enough? You measure it.

Experiment velocity: How many experiments does the organization run per month? Per week? Per day? This is a measure of learning throughput. Low velocity means the organization is learning slowly.

Experiment win rate: What percentage of experiments produce a statistically significant improvement? A very high win rate suggests the organization is testing only safe, obvious changes—and missing bigger opportunities. A very low win rate suggests the organization is testing randomly, without good hypotheses. The optimal win rate is in the middle (20-40% for most organizations).

Time from hypothesis to decision: How long does it take from the moment someone has an idea to the moment the organization knows whether it works? Short cycles mean fast learning. Long cycles mean slow learning.

Model freshness: How old is the production model? When was it last retrained? Stale models are inaccurate models.

Model improvement rate: By how much does model accuracy improve per retraining cycle? Diminishing returns are inevitable, but a flat improvement rate suggests the model has hit a plateau —or the retraining pipeline is broken.

Business impact: Ultimately, learning is measured by business outcomes. Are conversion rates improving? Are costs falling? Are customers more satisfied? Learning should translate to value.

Leaders should review these metrics regularly, just as they review financial metrics. Learning is not a soft capability. It is a hard driver of performance.

The Limits of Learning

Learning accelerates, but it is not infinite. There are limits.

Statistical limits: At some point, additional data yields diminishing returns. The model cannot be improved beyond the inherent predictability of the phenomenon. Some things are simply random.

Experimental limits: The organization cannot test everything. There are more possible changes than experiments that can be run. The organization must prioritize.

Organizational limits: Even with perfect experiments and perfect models, the organization must absorb the learning. It must change processes, retrain people, and update strategies. Organizational learning is the bottleneck.

Ethical limits: Not everything that can be tested should be tested. Experimenting on vulnerable populations, testing potentially harmful changes, or optimizing for metrics that conflict with human welfare—these are off limits. The learning system must have guardrails.

The wise leader recognizes these limits and does not chase impossible improvements. But between here and the limits is vast territory. Most organizations are nowhere near the frontier. The opportunity is enormous.

From Learning to Leading

The age of AI is the age of learning. The firms that learn fastest will lead. The firms that learn slowly will follow. The firms that do not learn will disappear.

Learning is not automatic. It requires investment: in infrastructure, in talent, in culture. It requires discipline: experimentation, measurement, iteration. It requires leadership: a CEO who prioritizes learning over comfort, evidence over opinion, speed over perfection.

The factory learns. The question is whether your factory learns faster than the competition.

A three-layer diagram showing the integration of model learning, experimental learning, and organizational learning:

Figure 14: The Learning Loop Integration

Below, a process flow for the experimentation loop:

Hypothesize → Configure → Execute → Analyze → Decide → Learn → (Repeat)

Chapter 15: Opportunities and Risks

The Double-Edged Sword

Throughout this book, we have painted a picture of extraordinary possibility. The AI Factory enables firms to scale without friction, learn without limit, and adapt without rewiring. It creates new revenue streams, delivers personalized experiences at scale, and drives operational efficiency that was unimaginable a generation ago. The opportunities are real, and they are transformative.

But the sword cuts both ways. The same capabilities that create value also create risk. The algorithms that personalize experiences can also encode bias. The data that powers learning can also be stolen. The platforms that enable scale can also concentrate power. The firms that win big can also lose everything if they fail to manage these risks.

This chapter provides a balanced assessment. We catalog the major opportunities—where the AI Factory creates value. We then examine the major risks—bias, cybersecurity, regulation, competitive dynamics—that threaten that value. And we offer a framework for navigating the trade-offs. The goal is not to dampen enthusiasm but to ground it in realism. The leaders who succeed will be those who seize the opportunities while managing the risks.

Part One: The Opportunities

Opportunity One: New Revenue Streams

The AI Factory opens revenue streams that were inaccessible under the old operating model.

Data monetization: Firms that collect valuable data can monetize it directly. Credit bureau data is sold to lenders. Purchase history data is sold to advertisers. Health data is sold to researchers. But data monetization is delicate—privacy concerns are real, and regulatory scrutiny is increasing. The most successful data monetization strategies are those where customers receive clear value in exchange for their data.

AI as a service: The capabilities of the AI Factory can be packaged and sold to other firms. Amazon sells its infrastructure (AWS). Google sells its models (Gemini API). Stripe sells its fraud detection. Any firm with a proprietary AI capability can consider whether that capability has value to external customers. This is the "picks and shovels" strategy for the AI age.

New business models: AI enables business models that were previously impossible. Usage-based pricing becomes feasible when real-time usage data is available. Dynamic pricing becomes feasible when demand can be predicted. Personalized subscriptions become feasible when preferences can be inferred. The AI Factory is not just a more efficient way to do old things. It is a way to do new things.

Product expansion: The strategic adaptability we described in Chapter 1 allows firms to enter adjacent markets by repurposing existing capabilities. A company that builds a logistics AI can expand into delivery, then into supply chain consulting, then into inventory finance. The AI Factory is a platform for growth, not just a tool for optimization.

Opportunity Two: Personalized Customer Experiences

Mass production delivered low cost but standardized products. The AI Factory delivers low cost and personalization.

Recommendation at scale: The classic application. Netflix recommends movies. Amazon recommends products. Spotify recommends music. Each recommendation is tailored to the individual user, based on their history and the history of millions of similar users. The result is higher engagement, higher satisfaction, and higher revenue.

Dynamic content: Beyond recommendations, AI can dynamically generate content tailored to each user. News feeds are ordered by predicted interest. Email subject lines are optimized for each recipient. Advertisements are personalized to the individual. The user sees what the algorithm predicts they will want to see.

Conversational AI: Chatbots and voice assistants provide personalized, real-time customer service. The AI knows the customer's history, anticipates their needs, and resolves their issues without human involvement. When escalation is needed, the handoff is seamless.

Predictive personalization: The most sophisticated personalization is predictive: the AI anticipates what the customer will want before they know it themselves. A grocery app adds items to the cart based on predicted needs. A calendar app schedules meetings based on predicted availability. A financial app saves money based on predicted cash flow. The customer experiences the brand as a partner, not a vendor.

The result is a virtuous cycle. Personalization increases engagement. Engagement generates more data. More data improves personalization. The firm that personalizes best learns fastest and wins.

Opportunity Three: Operational Efficiency

The AI Factory drives efficiency gains that dwarf traditional process improvement.

Automation of routine decisions: The most direct efficiency gain. Decisions that once required human judgment—credit scoring, fraud detection, inventory replenishment—are automated. The humans are redeployed to higher-value work. The cost per decision drops toward zero.

Optimization of complex systems: AI optimizes systems that are too complex for human analysis. Supply chains are optimized across thousands of products and hundreds of locations. Pricing is optimized across millions of products and billions of customer interactions. Logistics routes are optimized in real time based on traffic, weather, and demand. The efficiency gains compound.

Prediction as a substitute for inventory: In the industrial age, firms held inventory to buffer against uncertainty. In the AI age, better predictions reduce the need for inventory. A retailer that can predict demand with high accuracy holds less stock, reducing working capital and storage costs. A manufacturer that can predict equipment failure schedules maintenance just in time, reducing downtime and spare parts inventory.

Fraud and waste reduction: AI detects patterns of fraud and waste that humans cannot see. A health insurer identifies fraudulent claims. A retailer identifies employee theft. A government agency identifies improper payments. The savings are often substantial.

The cumulative effect of these efficiency gains is a structural cost advantage. The AI-native firm can offer lower prices, higher quality, or both—and still earn superior margins.

Part Two: The Risks

Risk One: Bias and Fairness

The most visible risk of AI is bias. Algorithms trained on historical data inherit historical biases. When those algorithms make consequential decisions—hiring, lending, sentencing—they perpetuate and amplify injustice.

Sources of bias: As we detailed in Chapter 12, bias can enter at any stage. Biased training data. Biased labels. Biased optimization objectives. Biased deployment contexts. The bias may be intentional (a firm that deliberately discriminates) but far more often it is unintentional (a firm that fails to notice that its model has learned discrimination).

Consequences of bias: The consequences are measured in human lives. A biased hiring algorithm denies opportunities to qualified candidates. A biased credit model denies capital to deserving entrepreneurs. A biased healthcare algorithm denies treatment to patients who need it. Beyond the human cost, bias creates legal liability, reputational damage, and regulatory scrutiny.

Mitigation: Mitigation is possible but not easy. Diverse data. Fairness constraints. Continuous monitoring. Human oversight. The organizations that take bias seriously invest in these mitigations. The organizations that do not will eventually be forced to.

Risk Two: Cybersecurity

The AI Factory runs on data. Data is valuable. Valuable assets attract thieves.

Data breaches: The most immediate cybersecurity risk. Customer data. Financial data. Health data. Proprietary models. All are targets. A breach can expose sensitive information, damage reputation, and trigger regulatory fines. The costs are measured in millions or billions.

Model theft: AI models are intellectual property. A competitor that steals your model can replicate your capabilities without your investment. Model theft can occur through breaches, through insider threats, or through model extraction attacks (where an attacker queries the model thousands of times to reconstruct its behavior).

Adversarial attacks: Models can be fooled. An adversarial example is an input deliberately designed to cause a model to make an incorrect prediction. A stop sign modified with stickers that cause a self-driving car to misclassify it. A transaction designed to evade fraud detection. Adversarial attacks are difficult to defend against because the attacker can adapt to the defender's countermeasures.

Poisoning attacks: If an attacker can inject malicious data into the training pipeline, they can poison the model. A poisoned model behaves normally most of the time but fails in specific ways chosen by the attacker. Poisoning is especially dangerous because the attack occurs before the model is deployed, making it difficult to detect.

Defense strategies: Defending the AI Factory requires a comprehensive security program. Encryption at rest and in transit. Access controls and audit logs. Intrusion detection and incident response. Adversarial training (training models on adversarial examples to make them robust). Continuous monitoring for unusual query patterns that might indicate extraction attacks.

Risk Three: Regulation

The era of unregulated AI is ending. Governments around the world are moving to regulate algorithmic systems.

The regulatory patchwork: There is no single global AI regulation. Instead, there is a patchwork of overlapping and sometimes conflicting rules. The European Union's AI Act is the most comprehensive, establishing a risk-based framework with strict requirements for high-risk systems. The United States has sectoral regulations (fair lending, employment discrimination, consumer protection) that apply to AI systems. China has regulations focused on algorithmic recommendation, deepfakes, and generative AI.

Compliance costs: Regulation imposes costs. Documentation requirements. Audit requirements. Reporting requirements.

Penalties for noncompliance. These costs are higher for smaller firms, creating a compliance barrier that favors incumbents.

Regulatory risk: The greatest risk is not the cost of compliance but the cost of noncompliance. A regulator that finds your AI system violates the law can impose fines, mandate changes, or shut down operations. The most aggressive regulators are in the EU, but other jurisdictions are following.

Navigating regulation: The smartest firms do not wait for regulation to be finalized. They proactively adopt responsible AI practices. They document their processes. They audit their models. They engage with regulators. They treat compliance as a feature, not a bug.

Risk Four: Winner-Take-Most Markets

The virtuous data cycle creates winner-take-most dynamics. A small number of firms capture the majority of market value.

The concentration dynamic: More users generate more data. More data improves the product. A better product attracts more users. The cycle reinforces itself. Competitors cannot catch up because they lack the data to train competitive models. The market concentrates.

The consequences of concentration: Concentrated markets have higher prices, less innovation, and less choice. The dominant firm has little incentive to improve because there is no competitive threat. New entrants cannot gain traction because they cannot match the incumbent's data advantage. The market stagnates.

The antitrust response: Regulators are increasingly concerned about AI-driven concentration. Antitrust enforcement is ramping up. The EU's Digital Markets Act imposes obligations on "gatekeeper" platforms. The US is considering similar legislation. The goal is to preserve competition without destroying the efficiencies of scale.

Navigating concentration: For incumbents, the risk is antitrust action. For challengers, the risk is being locked out. For both, the strategy is the same: build proprietary data advantages, but do not become so dominant that regulators intervene.

Risk Five: Platform Dependency

The AI Factory depends on cloud infrastructure, API services, and foundational models provided by hub firms. That dependency is a risk.

The concentration of infrastructure: Three firms—Amazon, Microsoft, Google—dominate cloud computing. If one of these firms raises prices, changes terms, or suffers an outage, thousands of dependent firms are affected. The dependent firm has little negotiating power.

API dependency: Many AI-native firms build on APIs provided by hub firms. OpenAI's GPT. Google's Gemini. Anthropic's Claude. These APIs can be changed or discontinued at any time. A firm that builds its entire product on an API that is later deprecated faces an existential crisis.

Data lock-in: Once a firm stores its data in a particular cloud provider's proprietary format, moving to another provider is expensive and difficult. The cloud provider knows this and can raise prices knowing that switching costs are high.

Navigating platform dependency: The defense against platform dependency is multi-cloud strategy (using multiple providers to avoid lock-in), open standards (avoiding proprietary formats), and building proprietary capabilities (not relying entirely on APIs for core value). The ideal is to use the hub firms for commodity capabilities while building proprietary advantage on top.

Part Three: Balancing Opportunity and Risk

The opportunities and risks are not separate. They are two sides of the same coin. The firm that seizes opportunities without managing risks will eventually fail. The firm that manages risks without seizing opportunities will be left behind.

The Trade-Off Framework

Leaders must navigate trade-offs across four dimensions.

Speed vs. Safety: Moving fast allows the firm to capture opportunities before competitors. But moving fast increases the risk of bias, security vulnerabilities, and regulatory violations. The leader must decide how much risk to accept in exchange for speed.

Personalization vs. Privacy: More personalization requires more data. More data increases privacy risk. The leader must decide where to draw the line. Some customers will trade privacy for personalization; others will not. The leader must understand the customer's preferences and respect them.

Efficiency vs. Resilience: Optimizing for efficiency reduces cost but creates brittleness. A supply chain optimized for lowest cost may have no slack when a disruption occurs. A cloud strategy optimized for lowest cost may rely on a single provider. The leader must decide how much redundancy to accept in exchange for efficiency.

Scale vs. Concentration: Scaling captures the benefits of the virtuous data cycle. But scaling also creates concentration, which invites regulatory scrutiny and may harm competition. The leader must decide how aggressively to scale and how to respond when regulators push back.

The Governance Response

The risks described in this chapter cannot be eliminated. They can only be managed. And management requires governance.

Risk management function: A dedicated team responsible for identifying, assessing, and mitigating AI risks. This team includes technical experts, legal experts, and policy experts. It reports to the CEO or the board.

Ethics review board: A cross-functional body that reviews high-risk models before deployment. The board includes members from engineering, product, legal, and policy. It has authority to block deployment.

Continuous monitoring: Risk is not static. New biases emerge. New vulnerabilities are discovered. New regulations are enacted. The organization must continuously monitor its risk posture and adapt.

Transparency and accountability: The organization must be transparent about its risk management practices and accountable for failures. This builds trust with customers, regulators, and the public.

The Strategic Response

Beyond governance, leaders must make strategic choices about which opportunities to pursue and which risks to accept.

Opportunity selection: Not every opportunity is worth pursuing. The firm should focus on opportunities where its capabilities are strong, the market is large, and the risks are manageable. Avoid opportunities where risks are high and mitigations are uncertain.

Risk transfer: Some risks can be transferred to third parties. Cyber insurance covers some security risks. Indemnification clauses in contracts transfer some legal risks. But not all risks can be transferred. Reputational risk, in particular, cannot be outsourced.

Risk acceptance: Some risks must be accepted. The firm that tries to eliminate all risk will never move. The leader must decide which risks are acceptable and which are not. This is not a technical decision. It is a value judgment.

The Path Forward

The age of AI is an age of extraordinary opportunity. The AI Factory enables firms to do things that were impossible a generation ago. New revenue streams. Personalized experiences. Operational efficiency. The potential is vast.

But the risks are equally real. Bias. Cybersecurity. Regulation. Concentration. Dependency. These risks can destroy value as quickly as opportunities create it.

The leaders who succeed will be those who embrace both sides of the coin. They will pursue opportunities aggressively but responsibly. They will manage risks systematically but without paralysis. They will build organizations that are powerful and principled, fast and safe, ambitious and accountable.

The factory does not rest. But it must be governed. The opportunity is too great, and the risk is too high, to do otherwise.

Figure 15: Balancing Opportunity and Risk

Caption: The AI Factory creates extraordinary opportunities—and equally significant risks. The wise leader does not choose one side over the other but actively balances both.

The Complete AI Factory — A Visual Summary

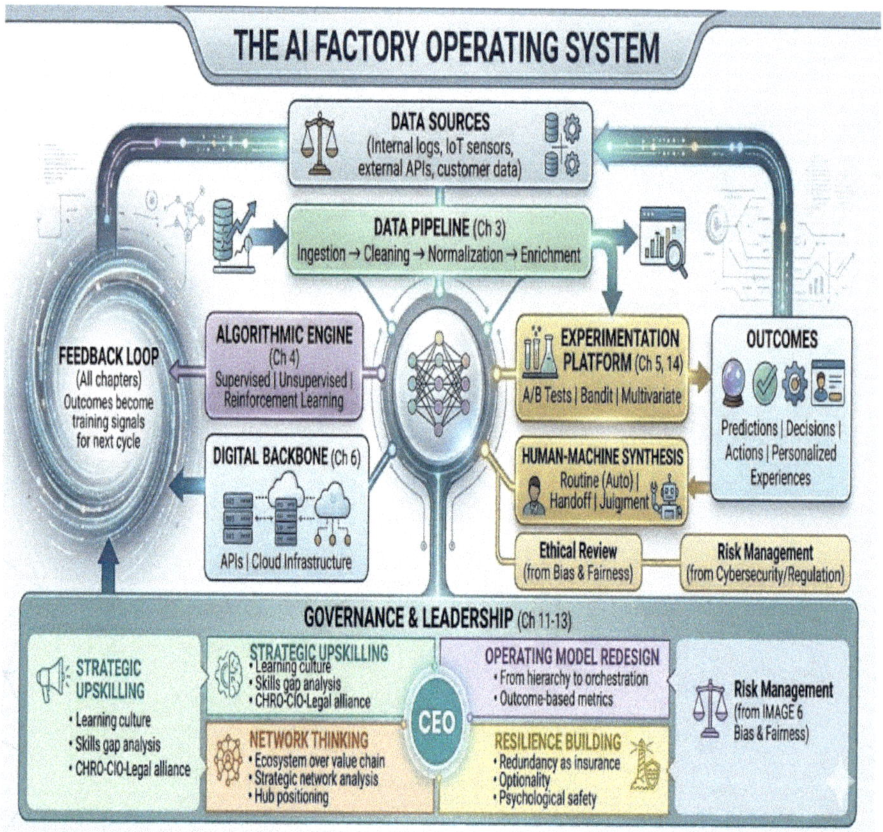

Figure : The AI Factory Operating System

Caption: The complete AI Factory operating system integrates data, algorithms, experimentation, infrastructure, human judgment, and continuous feedback—governed by ethical leadership at every layer.

Table of Contents

www.ingramcontent.com/pod-product-compliance
Lightning Source LLC
LaVergne TN
LVHW051102210926
848486LV00019B/404
* 9 7 8 2 3 8 2 2 6 6 7 0 0 *